Photo: Rycus Associates Photography/Michael A. Foley

PHYLLIS GREENE is a Phi Beta Kappa graduate of Wellesley College. She has had a lifelong involvement in her community, having served as chairman of the board of Franklin University, the United Community Council, and the Columbus Metropolitan Airport and Aviation Commission. In 2001, she was the recipient of the Columbus Metropolitan Library's Julian Sinclair Smith Celebration of Learning Award. She is the mother of three and the grandmother of eight. She lives in Columbus, Ohio.

It Must Have Been Moonglow

It Must Have Been Moonglow

Reflections on the First Years of Widowhood

Phyllis Greene

VILLARD Ⓥ NEW YORK

2003 Villard Trade Paperback Edition

Copyright © 2001 by Phyllis Greene

All rights reserved under International and Pan-American
Copyright Conventions. Published in the United States by
Villard Books, a division of Random House, Inc.,
New York, and simultaneously in Canada by
Random House of Canada Limited, Toronto.

VILLARD BOOKS and "V" CIRCLED Design are registered trademarks
of Random House, Inc.

This work was originally published in hardcover by Villard Books, a
division of Random House, Inc, in 2001.

Library of Congress Cataloging-in-Publication Data

Greene, Phyllis.
It must have been moonglow: reflections on the first years of widowhood / Phyllis Greene.
     p.   cm.
ISBN 0-8129-6784-4
1. Greene, Phyllis.   2. Widows—United States—Psychology—
Case studies.   3. Widows—United States—Biography.
4. Widowhood—United States—Psychological aspects—Case studies.   5. Bereavement in old age—United States—Case studies.
I. Title.
HQ1058.5.U5 G74 2001
305.48'9654'0973—dc21   2001026088

Villard Books website address: www.villard.com

Printed in the United States of America

987654321

Illustrations by Rosanna Fields
Book design by Carole Lowenstein

Here's to you, old dear

Robert B. Greene
March 7, 1915–December 12, 1998

Contents

It Must Have Been Moonglow

Just Another Widow

*T*HIS AFTERNOON, Mt. Carmel Hospice called for my six-month "checkup." How am I doing? they wanted to know. "Well," I said. "I am doing well." Am I telling the truth, I wondered; what is "well"? What sorrowing widow can ever really do well, I think. What standard does hospice use? With all their experience, they must have some definition of good and bad, well and unwell, heartsick and heartbroken. Of one thing I am sure: What is well one day is sick at heart the next, what is laughter one hour may be tears the next. In an effort to chart my own road to acceptance (I think it is there, some-where ahead), I began to keep a journal on December 31, three weeks after my husband's death. Now as I look back, I wonder if I have walked a mile or one hundred, if I am out in front or lagging way behind, if there is a "norm," and might it help me, and if there are others who may read this who would share my journey as I go? I would welcome the company.

Circles on the Third Floor

I AVOIDED WIDOWHOOD for fifty-six years. Bob and I tried really hard to make it longer than that, and he could have given up or given out any of the last ten, but he didn't. When he finally couldn't walk, or even move by himself; when I had to feed him and clean him; when he half-dreamed his own funeral and the "plaque" they would read, and the "people from Cleveland" who would come; when we could assure him that all the circles on the third floor were clean (although we have no third floor), then he and I and our internist knew it was finally time. The death certificate says the causes were cardiac arrest, arteriosclerotic heart disease, diabetes mellitus Type I.

What it was was that everything just deteriorated, ravaged by diabetes and age and the fact that his father, too, had died at eighty-three. So, in December 1998, I joined that unhappy band of women that has been growing like a geriatric sorority, and I became just another widow.

Looking back, all the way back to my teen years, I find so many different Phyllises as the years passed. I can see her, and almost feel her, but it is hard to get the true picture of what she was like as she moved forward (she hopes forward) through the physical changes and the cultural changes and the scientific and medical changes, through the feminist movement and the political upheavals. The one constant: for the last fifty-six years she has been Bob's wife.

All marriages have moments of great joy and great pain, the relationship changes over every decade, every day, and who I am now, who any of us are at the end of a marriage compared to who we were at the beginning is hard, even impossible, to get a handle on. I was a war bride, and while my husband was overseas I worked at a good and stimulating job as a fashion advertising copywriter for a department store. It was all new for me. I think there was a career, out in that exciting world, that we now call PR or media relations or marketing. But in 1945 I wanted none of that. I wanted a home in the suburbs and I wanted a baby. And then another and then another. We fit the statistical pattern perfectly: the house, the mortgage, the backyard barbecue, and my Major home from the war. A normal life, a conventional storybook, until suddenly it's time to write the last chapter.

What we always said to one another, especially as we came down the final stretch, was that we had had a helluva ride. This memory of our life that we ran over and over in our minds and conversations in the last year or two was the nourishment that gave us the strength to accept that it couldn't go on forever.

His Tan Poplin Suit and Repp Stripe Tie

*IT IS PAUL HARVEY who says "And now for the rest of the story," which is a good lead for breaking news. My story, actually, has no "rest," it just goes on and on. The rest of the story will evolve day by day, as long as I live.

I go through the necessary motions. I laugh some. I do shed some tears. I am learning to accept that this is the way it is, that there is almost nothing I can do except keep the faith, and walk through the storm with my head held high, and whistle while I work, and speak only soft answers to turn away wrath—and check my *Bartlett's Book of Quotations* for more clichés. For every widow there is a timetable, and "recovery" comes to each one on a different schedule and in a different way.

Just as recovering alcoholics are never free from the desire for a drink, so, too, am I, a recovering griever, never free of my desire for the life I had before. There just aren't any twelve steps that help. Nevertheless, with determination and reliance on the love and goodwill of friends and family, there are tolerable days and a window still on life's joys.

It seems incredible that months have passed and it is the bad memories of the last year of my marriage that are still so much clearer in my mind than the good memories of those many years that came before.

When I can reclaim those years, when the children were young and we lived in our lovely, traditional home, where we ate breakfast in a sunny breakfast room and ate dinner together every night, when Bob came home from work each evening to find his family awaiting his arrival, then I will know I am at least moving down that recovery road.

There is one picture in my mind of Bob that I return to over and over again. We are going out to dinner; his mother is here visiting us. We have driven to the top of the little hill and out of the driveway. Bob notices that he has forgotten to turn the pool sweep off, and so he goes down to turn the switch. As he comes back up the hill, in his tan poplin suit and his repp stripe tie and his blue button-down shirt, tan and healthy, with his great smile, I know that once and forever God is in his heaven and all is right with the world, my never-changing mantra.

When I say "Bob," and that is the picture that flashes into my mind and heart, then, perhaps, I can say that I am recovered.

Dear Diary

$\mathcal{F}$OR ME, the written word is the quintessential medium. From grocery lists to condolence messages to letters to friends or to the children at camp or for birthdays, it's the most effective way to express myself. Over the years, each time that Bob got sick, I would write a few words in the evening to remind me of how the day had gone. Each time he was in the hospital, I would come home and write. What was for me a tension release became, also, my medical log. By the time I had a computer, I had actual files of illnesses and operations, even one called Hive History, reporting when and how that chronic itch kept recurring. Bob got sick—really sick—the day after Labor Day, went to the hospital for tests and came home a bedridden, kidney-failing, medically complex, probably incurable, accepting good sport of a man. He died on December 12 after three horrible months that left us all heartbroken and devastated.

In the days after Bob's death, I gave no thought to writing anything other than thank-you notes for condolences. I was so busy, greeting visitors and talking to lawyers, talking to accountants, talking to the VA, being sure that we had someone to shovel snow. The mundane things were taking a lot of time.

As much as I enjoy writing, I would never have kept a daily journal after Bob died if I hadn't received my granddaughter Maggie's beautiful Christmas gift, a hardbacked journal, spiral-wire bound so that the lined pages lie flat for writing. On the cover there is the title *One Day at a Time* and a drawing of a lovely-looking older woman, in a big black hat, kneeling in her garden, tenderly holding a small plant in her hand, a not-so-subtle suggestion that she is probably a widow. The hat is the giveaway, that and the unmistakable sad expression. I got the message: Plant your small thoughts and they might help you heal and grow.

At first I thought it was a unique experience for me to find solace in writing my nightly entries. Once the tips-for-healing began arriving in the hospice mailings, it dawned on me that these journal jottings might be a comfort for others. Most of the published books I found about widowhood did not really speak to me; there were not many from a purely personal perspective. Thus, this book is just the journal, magnified. It is helping me even as I hope it helps those who might read it. We tackle our sorrow alone, but if we open ourselves with sympathy and empathy, it is a much less lonely road.

What started as a very private project began to take shape in my mind as something I could share, something for many of us, paddling away in the same small, sad boat.

Merchandise on State Street

NOT THAT LONG AGO, we, a couple, did what the funeral industry calls "preplanning." It required a weird combination of realism and common sense with a kind of denial that what we were doing was ever really going to be of any use. Die? Us? Of course we would—someday, someday—just not in our foreseeable future.

In November and December 1997 there was a promotion to plan and prepay your funeral, advertised by the Schoedinger Funeral organization, which has, for the last hundred years, buried almost everyone we know. If it didn't seem exactly a lark to go ahead and make these arrangements, it was not a depressing thing to do. In fact, everyone seemed to be doing it, saying at dinner get-togethers that they had been downtown to the State Street chapel to talk to Dave or Jay, the Schoedingers currently in charge. I had served on boards and committees with both of them, and Bob was a good friend and fellow Rotarian of the retired senior Schoedinger, John.

The rationale for doing this was to save our children some onerous decision making when they would be grieving. So down to State Street we went, and we filled out all the forms and even chose the "merchandise" (merchandise!): the casket, the urn, the cremation box. As we wandered around the second floor of the chapel, we thought it best not even to think of the implications, but just to get it done. And we did.

We chose a cemetery plot, too, and ordered headstones. And then it was all put in a file for what we hoped would be a long, long time. One year later, I pulled out the file for Bob, and his plan became operational.

We had assumed, I think, that there was a tax, as well as an emotional, advantage to all of this. There was, of course, neither. When it came time to list funeral expenses to be paid by the estate, we couldn't include the prepayment because it would have to be offset by the asset of owning the plan! If the prepayment was supposed to be a hedge against inflation, that didn't work for Bob, although it may for me. It came to be something that just was. Like the death itself.

I go to the cemetery now and am not sure I like the plot we chose, one of many that have belonged to my family for years. I know I do not like the headstone that bears both of our names. Somehow that macabre fact escaped me in the planning, but we have one grave, therefore one stone. At least my death date hasn't the inscription "19—," because 2001 is already here and, all things being equal, to have inscribed the wrong century for my death would have been bad planning indeed.

Is God in His Holy Temple?

THE END OF DECEMBER was a horror. Only able to capture memories of the last months, unable to bring up the old, happy ones, plagued by a real Midwest snowstorm that made our steep driveway impassable, and confronted, out of the blue, with another major family problem, I understood that death, alone, was not what was taking its toll.

Since then, I have witnessed this phenomenon over and over again. One widow came down with shingles, one's son lost his job, one's daughter got a divorce, one needed, immediately, to get a new roof. New widows begin to lose things: keys, canceled checks and the corresponding bank statements, even new checks to be deposited. If good things come in threes, bad things come in three times three.

When January 1 fell on a Friday, the first Friday since Bob's death that I could go to Temple, I knew it was time for some spiritual comfort in the house of the Lord. It was a brief service to welcome the Sabbath, held at 6:00 P.M. in the small chapel. The mini-sermon was taken from Genesis, about the death and burial of Jacob, with a meaningful message: *He lived.* What could have been a more appropriate way to say good-bye to the old year and try to welcome the new than remembering all the positive ways in which Bob had so boldly lived? Hundreds of letters and condolence cards, food, and flowers had demonstrated what we had always known, that the impression he left was vivid and lasting. To meet him once was to remember him with a smile. While I am not proud that organized religion and ritual have not played much of a role in our lives, I am grateful that God still occupies center stage. I envy those who find solace and shelter in their church, synagogue, or mosque. Although I seldom go to Temple, even on the High Holy days, I read the prayers to myself and feel comforted, a part of my people, all saying these same prayers on these same days all over the world.

The fall after Bob's death, however, I did feel the need to attend some of the services, particularly the memorial service on Yom Kippur, the Day of Atonement. So I sent for my tickets and received only one in the return mail. One ticket! I was angry all out of proportion. They hadn't cut my dues in half, so why reduce my ticket quota? I knew the answer before I asked: because there is only one of us now. It is a lesson that widows learn over and over but do not comprehend. We all may look the same in the eyes of the Lord, but in the temporal world, a widow does not look like a wife.

(The issuing of tickets for the High Holy Day services is peculiar to Judaism and is used to ensure that those who are current in their dues have a seat on the occasions when the Synagogues are likely to be filled to overflowing. Provisions are always made for hardship cases, of course.)

I went to the service anyhow, because I wanted to. I certainly didn't go because I thought Bob would have expected it of me. He would, in fact, have discouraged me. I could count the times on one hand that we had gone to Temple as a family. Well, maybe a few more if you count going to our children's confirmations. Once, Bob went when an expected hurricane missed Miami and his mother stayed out of harm's way. He did have a relationship with God, but it was in his own way and usually just in his own house.

When he lay dying, he said that he would like to talk to the Rabbi, and the Rabbi came twice to see him. There is but little solace that even a very skillful and caring man of the cloth can give a man or his family during the last days. Bob knew, though, that there had to be a peaceful way to go, and our Rabbi and our religion were going to help him do it.

Now, with the High Holy Days upon us, here I was at the traditional Memorial service for the bereaved. The service I remembered was so full of gloom; there was one passage that talked of our "moistening our morsel of bread with tears from the cradle to the grave." I hated to think of life that way. But the prayer book has been revised and the service was lovely and I was especially moved by the responsive reading that reminds us that "at the blowing of the wind and in the chill of winter, *we remember them;* at the opening of the buds and in the rebirth of spring, *we remember them;* at the blueness of the skies and in the warmth of summer, *we remember them;* when we are lost and sick at heart, *we remember them*" . . . and I did and do remember and am strengthened by those memories.

"So teach us to number our days that we may get us a heart full of wisdom" is another thing the psalmist says. I'm trying.

Like Mother, Like Daughter

$\mathcal{E}$VERY WIDOW FINDS OUT what every wife should know." I've heard that forever. My mother was twice widowed. I watched her take over my father's insurance business, and then remarry and sell the business so she could begin round two of the old-fashioned, stay-at-home life. She was able to make wise and generous decisions after she was widowed for the second time in twelve years and lived another twenty years alone. In many ways she was a remarkable role model, just as I guess her mother, widowed young, had been a role model for her. She was self-sufficient and independent, yet underneath that exterior, I (and I think I, alone) saw her anxieties and insecurities, many of which she covered so well that her demeanor made her seem daunting.

All through life, we all need support systems, especially women alone. We need a Rolodex of service people, we need a network of friends, and we need our children.

In the long, dreary months that Bob was sick, both of our sons and our daughter came when they were needed, but our young men had work obligations that didn't allow for extended stays. Our daughter, Debby, who is a writer, put her work on hold and came and stayed for the duration. In fact, she came and stayed for life, moving back to her hometown, buying a house near me, and resuming her career from a new base. Looking back, I am not sure how I would have managed without her. The computer and the telephone are great communication tools, but seeing and touching are better! We have always had a fine mother-daughter relationship, and in that I have always felt blessed. These days we are best friends. Yet I worry that the time could come when she will become the parent, and I will no longer be co-equal but a dependent. I remember precisely when it happened with my mother. When she could no longer manage her own checkbook, I began paying her bills, and then making first minor then major decisions. By the time she died, her children had become management consultants, full-time advisers and advocates.

I have been talking to an out-of-town friend who has been an exemplary daughter to parents who are both well into their eighties. For years they lived in a different state, but she recently moved them to her town, in their own apartment. And now, lo and behold, the dynamic has changed between the mother and daughter, because the good daughter has found the load too heavy to bear. She is, in the vernacular, fed up. Because it has lasted too long? Because it is now so inescapable? Each of them is evaluating her own role as they work to re-establish the special relationship they once had. What we all need to do when these emotional and spiritual crises arrive is to remember the old adage "This too shall pass," and the even older one "True *filial* love conquers all."

We have always been a family of constant communication and today it is more constant than ever.

Talking to my sons is a tonic. They still consider me a fully functioning being who is interested in both their joys and their problems. My grown children are my first line of defense against anxiety and insecurity, and it is our mutual dependence that makes me feel that I am still in control of my world. I realize, however, that if my mother, of all people, could become a very dependent older woman, so, too, can I.

Tim once bought a beautiful little book to read to his three-year-old son, and it was so moving for him that he bought a copy for me. It's called *Love You Forever*, by Robert Munsch. Tucker is now fifteen, and so it has been beside my bed for twelve years. It gets truer by the day. The first page shows a young mother rocking her baby, singing softly that he will always be her baby, and that she will always love him.

It then follows the boy through the terrible twos and disrespectful nines and the crazy teens and still, each night, the mother creeps into her son's room and holds him and sings. Eventually he grows up, moves across town, and has a house of his own. Still, at night, she drives over and holds him and sings the same song to him. When she grows too old, and can no longer drive to him, he drives to her and he creeps into her room and sings to her. This year, when Tim came for Thanksgiving, I was just out of the hospital with my new pacemaker. His helping Debby with the Thanksgiving dinner, including polishing the fancy salt and peppers, buying a new shower curtain for the downstairs bathroom, and closing the water lines for winter were Tim's way, we both knew, of singing the song to me. When you near the end of the book, when the balance of responsibility shifts, we need to accept graciously.

Though you hate to admit it, when you realize that being taken care of is not all bad, those are the times when children might know best. I think all of us have had the subtle message from our loving offspring that, perhaps, we are trying to do too much without their assistance. Just as A. A. Milne's James James Morrison Morrison Weatherby George Dupree said to his mother, so, too, do we get the subliminal message (prefaced kindly by "How many times do I have to tell you?"), "Don't ever go down to the end of the town if you don't go down with me." Have I bought the right suit? Did I call the right plumber? Should I have fired the grass cutter? These are everyday, simple choices that you could easily make for yourself, but a little input is reinforcing. After all, you have fifty-six years' experience as a partner in decision making. But when you escalate from the humdrum to the meaningful—from lawn care to law care, from stockings to stocks—these are the times for a good, two-way communication with your children.

At Wellesley College, the college motto is evident everywhere; engraved not only in stone but in the heart of every graduate: *Non Ministrari, sed ministrare,* not to be administered unto but to administer. Absorbed as if by osmosis, it has become a guiding principle of my life. From the little and unimportant decisions to major challenges, I wanted to be the doer, not the done for. I preferred to drive the car pools; I prefer now to manage my own financial affairs, or at least choose my advisers. In that, I am indeed my mother's daughter. What I live in fear of becoming is my mother . . . being administered unto.

On-the-Job Training

LIKE MOTHERHOOD, there are rules for widowhood that you are supposed to grasp instinctively, and like motherhood, we all learn on the job the first time around. Instinctively, you know that you should say "fine" when anyone inquires how you are doing. (For a few months, I said, "Fine, but it's crappy," and then even I got tired of hearing that.) Instinctively, you know you can open up to another widow better than half of a couple; instinctively, you take on the jobs that need doing: the checkbooks, the financial decisions, the home maintenance. What once worried your husband, and which you were inclined to shrug off—urging him *not* to care if the electrician didn't show up or the stock market wavered or you had accepted an invitation when you really didn't want to go—is now your responsibility alone and there is no one to complain to when any of it goes wrong. There is, of course, another side of this: You don't have to justify the mistake you made in the checkbook, or the fact that you actually called the electrician when all you had to do was check the fuse box, or that you, out of hand, decided that it was time to sell a stock that had been doing nothing (and then, within weeks, was part of a very profitable merger deal!). "Those things happen" you say to nobody but yourself.

Because you do talk to yourself. A lot. Or to the missing husband. Many an evening, as I pour a glass of wine, I find myself saying, "Let's have a drink, it's five o'clock, Bob," and I can actually conjure up his presence. I look over at his chair and raise my glass and say, as I always did, "Here's to you, old dear," and almost see him. In the night, too, I instinctively look over at his bed to listen for his breathing. How often I reassured myself in our later years just by listening at 2:00 A.M. It is heartbreaking and comforting all at once. I know widows who rail at their husbands, asking why they had left them alone, angered at the abandonment, frustrated by the burden. There are times when talking out loud, to the missing mate or just to yourself, makes the house less quiet. When all the chores are done before ten in the morning (make *the* bed, wash *the* dish), then the stillness descends and the day stretches long ahead. There are days when the stillness is so still that I hear a clock ticking even when there is no clock in the room. Some widows run to errands or lunches or lectures, great escapes in some cases. Others find it is easier to stay home, stay in, stay unpressured. Whichever you choose, you better like your own company, for run though you may, there is no running from your widowhood. How ironic that *it* is a constant companion. Still and all, I have come to be a true believer in the utter necessity for a widow to get on with life. Your heart may feel like stone but your mind needs to keep going.

After Bob retired, we usually spent the three cold Ohio months on Longboat Key, on the west coast of

Florida. One year I elected to take a course at The Education Center, a continuing education kind of facility in a pleasant suite of rooms above the Centre Market. A diversified curriculum in four- and seven-week sessions was offered, something for the early snowbirds who came for many months as well as those there only for a short visit. The geriatric students could choose ethics or literature or bridge, art or music or psychology. The west coast of Florida has an abundance of retired professors, as well as current academics at nearby colleges, and classes filled rather quickly. Our class, which met once a week on Thursday morning, I think, had overtones of feminism (feminism for the senior citizen) called Women and Agelessness, which I considered a very diplomatic touch. (It could have been titled Women and Aging just as easily!) The reading list was not required, which was fortunate, because Andrew Carnegie never did find Longboat Key, but some good books were available at the volunteer-run library near Town Hall. The first session was "Woman's Journey Through the Life Cycle," and readings were from Carolyn Heilbrun, Deepak

Chopra, and, of course, Betty Friedan. What began that morning was an opening up among twelve women with our age as our common denominator. Our teacher/discussion leader was a retired Ph.D., a former dean of the School of Consumer and Family Sciences at Purdue. She was a widow who was well traveled and excellent at leading a group and keeping them pretty much on track, though we did, of course, have one member who tended to get carried away by the sound of her own voice. What I remember most clearly from our seven weeks together was the change that these few hours seemed to have made in the life of one participant, a very recent widow who came to the first class weeping, hardly able to introduce herself. Each week she revealed a little more of herself. I wish I could say that by the end of the course she was a barrel of laughs. What I can in truth report is that the sense of camaraderie among this group of strangers offered her a feeling of composure and brought her the knowledge that there is life after widowhood.

There are, of course, invitations to go out. Lunches are easy; there is no problem about paying your own way. Dinner is another matter. In the paternalistic society in which we all grew up and grew older, when going out as a couple, the gentleman pays the bill, but after a number of times being on the receiving end of this, you want to pay your share— and you meet resistance. I know a woman who has learned to say, very authoritatively but quietly, when the waiter asks for her order, "I would like a Beefeater martini and my own check, please." Sometimes that works. Another friend solves this by entertaining quite often in her home, which is lovely, but having people for dinner is not as easy as it once was. Getting the food on the table is not half as hard as cleaning it up afterward.

When we were a couple and had brought a widow to a party, I was very aware that she had to accommodate herself to our schedule. Not fair, but that seems to be the way it works: You have to be ready to be picked up (and wait by the window for your friends to fetch you); if they are late, you are late. When you are one of a couple and want to leave a party, just the raising of an eyebrow is a signal between two long-married people. You, the widow, are not entitled by these new rules to be the eyebrow raiser. Even in leisure activities, you are hostage to your widowhood.

Then there is the problem of night driving. I was a novice at it because whenever we went anywhere together, Bob absolutely insisted that he be the driver, day or night. The only times he ever let me drive were coming home from the hospital. Even the summer afternoon when he tripped in the driveway, bleeding profusely from both arms and both legs, *he* drove to the doctor. I had to run into the office and get a nurse to come with a wheelchair. It was almost embarrassing to have him get out from behind the wheel. Yet it was important to his self-esteem to be the driver, even though I often felt I might be taking my life in my hands to sit there beside him. Now that I have the option, I like counting on myself. One of the rules of widowhood seems to be that when there is a car full of women, it is the shortest route to the party or the restaurant that dictates who will drive— among the able-bodied. There is no sense to go west to pick someone up if the destination is east. That western widow gets the duty. So it has happened that on the night of a torrential thunderstorm, the job has fallen to the widow with incipient macular degeneration, and the night of an unexpected snowstorm, I was driving, and the night when the trip was the longest, the driver was the one with the worst sense of direction. All of us welcome daylight savings time and 9:30 P.M. sundowns.

A friend, who was widowed young, made a conscious decision that she did not want to go out with women-only groups. She was fortunate that many of her contemporaries were still couples and happy to include her, but an older widow who thinks she can divorce herself from widows in bunches does so at a potential cost. The high cost of loneliness.

There is an old and fairly tired joke about the widower who told his friend that he was going to be married. "Oh," said the friend, "I'm happy for you. Is she young?" No, came the answer. Then, "Is she pretty?" No. "Is she rich?" No. "Is she sexy?" No, again. "Then why," asks his friend, "are you marrying her?" And the answer: "Because she drives at night." When I first heard it, I hardly got it. But now that I truly understand it, it is painful in its implications. If you are fortunate enough to have the capability of driving at night, and you really want to go somewhere, you can. But if you cannot drive at night (or even in the day, for that matter), you are indeed isolated.

An old friend recently called from Hawaii to see how I was doing. We had a lovely talk and he told me that he and his wife were coming to California for a vacation, and while there, his wife was going to her sixtieth high school reunion. Guess what time it will be held? he asked. Twelve noon. He told me because it *is* a funny time for a party. But, of course, he still drives at night.

Time and Change

I won't be eating dinner in the kitchen or dining room. It's lonely.

Nothing is messed up or out of place.

Cleaning drawers and closets is more a time-killer than a chore.

Our bedroom is neat all the time.

When I wake up at night, I can turn the light on if I want to—
but I don't. I even walk to the bathroom in the dark.

I will be driving at night.

I have too many towels and wash rags—and hardly any laun-
dry loads.

I only buy a quart of milk at a time and that goes sour before I
use it up.

Finally, I think of a plus; I am in control of the remote . . . and I
don't have to watch the History Channel.

I can eat when I want and don't have to (get to) think about
  blood sugar and insulin.

When you live in Columbus, Ohio, *time and change* are not just three words. Even if you did not attend The Ohio State University, you know the alma mater, sung at every game, including the words "time and change will surely show, how firm thy friendship, O-HI-O." As I consider this giant change in my life, that phrase keeps resonating, and I guess what I am wishing, with all my aching heart, is that time will make me accepting of the change. That I, with time, will accept the change.

In myriad small ways, the whole gets changed. Not just the big, dramatic major catastrophe of it all, but something in every hour of every day is different from before. It's an old cliché that the sum of the parts often add up to more than the whole . . . and in this case, the sum of the hole makes it a gigantic chasm. It's a feeble joke but one that I visualize, when I drive home from an evening with friends at 11:00 P.M. I know that Bob, from somewhere, is watching me, furious that I am alone in the car at that hour and anxious for me to turn into the garage.

Sleeping habits change, too. I often doze off as I am reading in bed, and sleep with the light on for maybe an hour. When I awake, I turn the light off. Then, if I can't sleep, I read some more. Or I sleep until 2:30 A.M., when I begin to read again for an hour. I would never have been so unstructured with Bob in the other bed.

If sleeping is a changing pattern, eating is even more so. For almost forty years, we were on a strict regimen; breakfast at 8:00 (blood sugar at 7:30), lunch at 12:00, and dinner at 6:00 (blood sugar, of course at 5:30). When we strayed from the schedule there was always an insulin reaction to contend with. Now, I don't even have orange juice in the house, or peanut-butter crackers.

There is the question of the beauty parlor, too. I have always had my hair "done" on Friday; so did my mother before me. Before Bob got so sick, I had a standing appointment that was written in the appointment book months and months ahead—and being written in a beauty parlor's appointment book is really the same as being written in the proverbial stone. But now I am thinking of changing my appointment to Monday. The weekend is much quieter than the week. Who is to see me many weekends except Gwen Ifill or Louis Rukeyser? If a friend and I want to see a movie and have dinner, how often are Friday or Saturday or Sunday all available choices?

Even my taste buds seem to react differently. Once, a good cup of coffee in the morning was the only way to start the day. Recently, I have tried every brand they sell, literally, and they all taste terrible to me. I have switched to tea, which, formerly, was reserved for 4:00 P.M. when I would so often ask Bob, "Would you like a nice cup of tea?" and he would invariably ask me, "Is *nicecuppa* a brand name?"

In clothes, I tend to prefer beige and gray and black. I don't mean to limit my color palette so; red and orange and the brights look unbecoming. Why? I'm not shopping for widow's weeds, of course. Just age-appropriate or mood matching or whatever. So I remind myself that, when I look around, at people in general and of any age, it seems that what matters more is the look you have on your face, not the clothes you have on your back. I buy smaller sizes for my incredible, shrinking self, I buy bigger purses since I have no one to carry the compact or lipstick I often asked Bob to put in his pocket. Never before was I the keeper of the keys.

This may sound very gloom and doom, which is not my take on life at all. I hate being alone and living alone, but I am not depressed. I think I might even be clinically described as "pretty happy." David Myers, who has written a book entitled *The Pursuit of Happiness: What Makes a Person Happy and Why*, says that "there are genetic predispositions to happiness. I liken happiness to cholesterol levels: Both are genetically influenced and yet both are, to some extent, under our control." So just as I take Pravachol for my cholesterol, so, too, do I try to keep a supply of optimism and good perspective at hand, plus a backup of as much of a sense of humor as I can muster.

Safe at Home

SAFETY IS NOT something with which I have ever been terribly concerned. In the good old days, when we hadn't all become so frightened and suspicious, when, to be honest, there was so much less to be frightened and suspicious about, we always kept our back door unlocked so that the milkman could look in the refrigerator and put in whatever he thought we needed. I often left my purse in my grocery cart while I went elsewhere in the store to look for something. I sometimes still do.

Or rather, I did. *Did.* Not now, not after what happened this week. I went to the underappreciated supermarket, happy to be allowed to drive after recovering from the addition of my pacemaker. It had been a month since I had been able to do my own shopping, and I almost enjoyed the leisurely meander up and down the aisles. At the meat counter, some beautiful, fresh stewing beef caught my eye. (I must have been stir-crazy if I can describe beef as "beautiful.") Having bought the beef, I went looking for Wyler's Soup Starter, a good and tasty and very easy way to make (almost) homemade vegetable soup. (First you brown the beef cubes, then you add water, then you toss in the soup mix, and an hour and a half later—well, Julia Child would be proud.) The mix was in the soup aisle, as always, but it was on the top shelf. A pleasant-looking thirty-something woman reached it down for me, and then began to discuss the sodium content of various instant cubes and granules. I am open and certainly not wary of talking to strangers in a grocery. She told me that she couldn't read, so I, sympathetic to anyone deprived of a good education (of whom we have too many in Columbus), helped her read the labels and we must have examined products for two or three minutes. At one point, I thought I felt a movement near me, but I quickly glanced back and saw my purse just where I had left it, in the cart basket that's the child-carrying seat. Shortly thereafter, a man reached across in front of me to get a can of soup and said, "I'm looking for some sodium-free soup," and I smiled as I replied, "That's just what we were talking about." He smiled back and for that brief second, I thought we three strangers had shared a lovely moment of human communication. Then he left, she left, and I picked up a box of shredded wheat and headed for the checkout. When I opened my wallet, I was horrified to find my Visa card and Discover card were gone from their usual top slots. My cash was intact. I had been snookered, scammed, taken for what I obviously am: a vulnerable older person. I wanted to call the credit card companies *asap*, but the number to reach them to report a stolen card is on the back of the card itself! The checkout girl said she thought it also was on the monthly statement. I flew home and went straight for my records, but no luck. I called 411, except I didn't know where Discover or Chase Gold Visa would be located and I felt stumped and stupid. With each passing minute I could see those two on a great shopping spree. Suddenly, I remembered seeing Bob's wallet in his top dresser drawer and, in it, his cards. I called the numbers, pressed one, pressed two, kept pressing and waiting and finally found a live person to report the theft. Saved again, by Bob. I wasn't even surprised. Discover told me that my husband could not use his card. I explained his death and so the new card was reissued to me alone. I had just never bothered to change the account from his name to mine. Visa was not so easy. I had to speak to a special unit that handles such delicate matters (rather indelicately, I think). They sent me paperwork that I had to complete before becoming a widow in Chase's eyes. To prove it, I had to include a copy of the death certificate.

Bob always thought we ought to be aware of life's dangers. I knew he had a gun that he had brought home from the war, but he certainly didn't have it anywhere that I knew about and it certainly had no bullets. Though we almost never mentioned its existence, it was a kind of mental security blanket for him. After he died, when I was cleaning out his desk,

I came across a broken pistol, the one captured from a dead German soldier, I think. I threw it in the trash. Then, cleaning out the shirt drawer, I found *another* gun and I called the police to come get it. It was a Sunday and they were too busy for my pitiable little errand, but told me to call the next day. The officer I talked to that time told me not to give it to them, because they would just melt it down. I should call an antiques dealer. "It sounds like it's valuable," she said. With the blessing of the police and a referral, I reached a dealer who said it was likely worth a hundred dollars. Would I bring it to him? Money is money, but I would not drive across town with a gun in my car for twice that. The dealer came to me and gave me fifty bucks, exactly what he had folded in his pocket and knew I would settle for. In all likelihood, it was the broken German gun that was valuable, but for me, neither of them had any future in my life. Guns are surely not the way to a safe life, but now I am having to figure out what is.

(*Not too much later it was reported on the news that, indeed, the police sell to dealers who sell to the public, one of whom was a young boy who went to Columbine High School! What can Messers. Heston and LaPierre be thinking?*)

Safety, of course, means more than fear of an intruder. Increasingly, I feel that it means fear of too many stairs, too many moving of hoses, too much repainting of doors, too many worn appliances. Our house sits midway down a small hill; the road is above us in the front, and the yard and pool are down in back. This makes for a steep drive down to the garage and a hard climb up to the mailbox. That's a minus. When you enter the house from the garage or the front door, the whole first floor opens up to you. As you walk down the hallway to my bedroom, though, it becomes the second floor, perched as it is above the other part of the downslope. And so I feel safe. That is a plus. There is a lower level as well, reached by steps that I have come to dread. Too much house for one, but because I am that one, it feels just right. The thought of moving to a one-floor plan that would make entry much more accessible to anyone is definitely a minus.

There are some lovely condominium/houses in a new development next to me. I have looked at them three times. Tim and Debby have seen them with me. I thought then (and I think I think now) that I am not ready. But the Ohio drought is for real; this year's impatiens are completely dead; the grass, they say, will come back, but it looks awful; all the planting up by the mailbox has been pulled out. I know that all I need do is swallow hard and pay the bills and realize that I love my house. The problem is that it is getting to be a love/hate relationship. We have lived in this house almost thirty years in peaceful coexistence with nature, and I have been primarily a spectator at the sport of tending the yard and flower beds and pool. (I was, however, a great weed-puller.) Now, too often, I feel beset by the twin demons: the driveway in winter, the pool in summer. Although I truly believe in the equality of the sexes, I would wager that there is no older woman alone who doesn't need a handy (type) man.

I was thinking this evening, as I was moving the hose yet again, how much I have always loved summer. It was my favorite season, thriving on the sunshine, the warmer the better. Now, I search for every little rain cloud that could mean that I might put off watering the grass for another day.

The August before Bob died, the entire family gathered for a reunion that I called "our very own millennium." Was I tempting fate, or did we know that it was the last time the family Greene would all be together? Shortly after that, Bob had the fractured sacroiliac, then he tripped in the driveway, and from then to Labor Day it was a steady downhill slide. So there were many months when he was still living that there was little he could do physically and nothing that he would allow me to do. "Don't go down those stairs, Phyl" or "Don't worry about the dishwasher." He wanted to make things as easy for me as he could, but I am not sure how to make things easy for myself. We often talked of moving from here together, and even looked at some places. The enormity of the job made us sit back and say that we would never move. I'm still juggling those options in my head.

A Trust/
B Trust/
No Trust

WHEN JAMES CARVILLE made such a big deal (and a president) out of his theme "It's the economy, stupid," I thought it was just a smart-ass, PR man's slogan. Not so. What it is is plain smart . . . because everything is, of course, the economy.

It is an overriding concern for the widow, whatever her fiscal situation. From the widow who scrimps to get by to the widow with extra cash to invest, there are hard choices to make. And it is the hard choices in life that keep us tossing and turning at three in the morning. The most long-lasting lesson I learned from *King Lear* is that it's easy to choose between good and bad; it's choosing between good and good or bad and bad that will get you every time.

I was in the grocery last week, and a lovely-looking older woman was checking out in front of me. Her obvious physical disability was osteoporosis, but she looked comfortably middle-class with blue-rinsed hair and a companion to help with the marketing. But what struck me was the number of food coupons she had clipped and used for her shopping, and how plaintively she asked the clerk if the total owed included a $10 discount to which she was entitled. We all need to be careful shoppers, but this looked like more than "care" to me, and I thought of the choices she had made to set her priorities. Had she just gotten her hair done because a grandchild was coming to visit? Was the "companion" actually a neighbor, helping out? Was she living on a very fixed income, shopping with care, or just naturally frugal, a woman who remembers the Great Depression and can never be profligate with her spending?

We had a friend, some years ago, whose father was always nervous about spending money. He was not wealthy, but certainly comfortable enough. He lived in a hotel and did not drive. In addition, he liked to play poker. So he held his cash (and his cards) close to the vest. He wouldn't take a taxi, but rode the bus to the country club so that he could play. As we get older we all have very understandable fears about outliving our money. In this era of astronomical health care costs, especially long-term health care, like the lady with the blue hair, we are afraid of the choices we may have to make not only for our own well-being but to be able to leave something beside good memories to our children.

A Wellesley song of long ago (and probably still) talks about the seniors (senior class, that is) "safe now, in the wide, wide world." How welcoming that world looked on the steps of the chapel in 1941. Truly, how at home I have always felt in the wide, wide world. But the sense of responsibility I feel now not only for my well-being but for preserving all that Bob worked a lifetime for, to pass on to the children . . . no magazine article can walk me safely down that road. Even with the help of financial planners and advisers, I feel very alone making the kinds of decisions that Bob and I always made together.

Money is a very personal topic, yet I have revealed more about my financial situation to more people than I ever thought I would. The discussion begins with the philosophical questions, and once you begin to talk about your priorities (whether to preserve as much as you can for the grandchildren or, conversely, "let the grandchildren fly tourist"), often, you then find yourself discussing philanthropy, or travel, or risk investments. And when you go home from the lunch or the dinner, you wish you could say, "Bob, you won't believe how much D seems to have, or how close to the edge E is living." And you wonder how much private information you have revealed without meaning to.

It has been a number of months now since I became solely responsible for all decision making. I have made many major choices, recognizing that sometimes not doing anything is a choice in and of itself. During these last months, with the whole of my future, and of our family, resting in my hands, I have had to say yes or no on the route we should take. We are still upright, and whether I have been wise or stupid, what needed to be done has been done.

Watch Out for Booby Traps

DOING WHAT you have to do, making decisions that need making—those are in your control. You know that you are in charge. But you never know when you are going to be blindsided. I try to defend myself against it by surrounding myself with things that might knock me out if I came on them unawares.

Just to the left side of my computer, on the wall, there is a long frame with three pictures. The top is the completed needlepoint piece that my mother had seed-stitched from the colored chart that is the bottom picture that my daughter had made from the actual photograph in the middle of my mother, my daughter, her daughter, and me. And stuck in the frame's edge is a photo taken at a country club, our neighbor June's daughter's wedding in 1968. There we are: June and another couple and Bob and I, in our evening clothes, drinks in hand, all of us looking so young, so happy, so much a part of the busy world. Because I see these photographs many hours of every day, I can view them with happiness. If I came on them unaware—oh, it would be unbearable.

Which is why it is better for me to try to prepare myself for all the eventualities that can rise up and hit me smack in the face. I remember when my niece Molly was married, not too long after my mother had died. My mother, like Bob, had been more than ready to go—aged, ill, lonely, her days were a burden she was anxious to relinquish. It was when Molly's other grandmother, Sug, was being escorted down the aisle to be seated that the sobs that I had not shed at the funeral (or since) absolutely overwhelmed me. Out of left field. I could not stop them any more than I could have stopped the death itself. These are the moments you try to prepare for, but of course, you cannot.

Recently, Van Cliburn was in town to play with

the Columbus Symphony Orchestra and a very nice friend asked me to go. I knew that I would vividly recall an earlier evening, an evening that was memorable for the few of us who were invited to attend a lovely, late, after-concert supper in honor of Mr. Cliburn and his mother. They arrived later than the rest of us because they had other postconcert obligations. We had nothing to do but have some hors d'oeuvres, some drinks, and begin to have fun. Bob sat down at the piano to make a little music before the real musician arrived! However, the only song he knew how to play was "Moonglow," and he did leave the piano when the guests of honor arrived. But as the hour grew later, the thought of playing for Van Cliburn was just so overwhelmingly attractive that our always irreverent friend Harry wrote a note, addressed to the host, saying "Please let Bob Greene play 'Moonglow' "—and got the magnanimous virtuoso, Van Cliburn, to sign it. The host and Mother Cliburn were not amused, but all the rest of us happy heartlanders found it uproarious. Which explains the *New Yorker* cartoon I keep on my bulletin board, showing a middle-aged, midwestern, midsophisticated couple driving home, obviously from a party, the husband singing to the wife. The caption underneath reads: "It must have been moonglow, up in the blue. It must have been moonglow, that brought me straight to you." Among the songs played at Bob's funeral: "Moonglow." Our own hymn.

There are phrases that trigger memories, too, phrases that you haven't even thought about but that mean more to you than the actual words. I often hear myself saying "Can I ask you a favor," something Bob always said before he asked, or "If it wouldn't be too much trouble" or, when someone asks what we should do for entertainment today or tonight, "we could go jezz bend densing," and the ultimate approval of a friend: "He speaks the language." When, inept as I am with a screwdriver, I think to myself, "I can't get purchase," that is Bob at his most precise, and when I close the windows and turn on the air-conditioning, I think, "Hotter than a popcorn fart," Bob at his least eloquent. Definitely his vocabulary, now mine.

And names in the paper, too. I read Bighouse or Daughters or Pfleuger, old army names or Akron names, people I didn't know but who meant so much to Bob. These, of course, are not the same Sergeant Bighouse or "Grandma" Daughters or Johnny Pfleuger. Yet I know that the memories triggered by these names would mean so much to Bob. I have inherited those memories. How great that the IRS can't get to them.

More than once, in the last months, there has also been the booby trap that is toughest of all. Those who do not know of his death always ask when they see me, "How's Bob?" He was so friendly and well-liked that younger men, especially, who know me only to say hello, really warmed to him. It is the most natural question in the world. It is hard for them when I have to say that he died in December, so I cover for them; I almost apologize. I explain how sick he was, that it was time, what a helluva ride we had for fifty-six years. They are embarrassed and I am uncomfortable and very surprised. From the numbers of people who sent condolences and contributions, I thought *everyone* knew.

That innocuous-looking TV set can floor you, too. There is an eyeglass commercial for lenses that change from light to dark and the music played is "I'll be seeing you in all the old familiar places." I have learned to push the mute button practically before the first note. It breaks my heart.

ABC had a special called "Influences." It showcased various TV stars of today who have been influenced by those of the past, and, of course, those past stars were *our* stars. So Dennis Franz was influenced, he says, by Jackie Gleason and Kelsey Grammer by Jack Benny and Matt Groening by the "Leave It to Beaver" show. Conan O'Brien was scheduled to refer to Sid Caesar in the last half hour, but I had to turn the TV off. The whole two hours was a knockout, blindside punch. Seeing the clips of all our favorite shows, I could hear Bob laugh as I sat there watching alone. Watching what he not only loved the first time around, but realizing just how much he would have enjoyed these reminiscences sent me to the shower. Better to get in bed and read a book and not rub salt into the wound.

Holidays are a wound of their own. At Christmas and New Year's this year, I was still numb. On the Fourth of July, which was always our traditional ingathering, we in-gathered once again, and it was hard on us all. I know we all have to celebrate my eightieth birthday. My choice would be to put my head in a sack, go into a coal mine, and emerge, ready for the eighty-first—and not look back. Instead, we planned for us all to go to Chicago and pretend that we were having fun. This Labor Day is not only a holiday but an anniversary: It was the day after Labor Day that I called Dr. Shell to tell him that Bob was deteriorating in front of my eyes, and then we called the squad to take him to the hospital, where he heard the medical results that sentenced him to death. It is Labor Day weekend as I write, and it is the longest weekend ever.

Don't Dizzy Me Around

*T*OO MANY THINGS GO WRONG—not big things, just the daily screwups. Some are my fault, some actually do have to do with the state of the service industry in this country. But each time there is another unnecessary problem to fix, I invariably say, "It's a disgrace." It was a disgrace when Debby's out-of-town realtor made an error in the valuation of her house; it was a disgrace when the bank lost my deposit (and another bank would not help me balance my checkbook, though I had been a customer since Bob went overseas in 1945, and my numbered checks were up to #15600). It got so I thought that if the grocery didn't carry capers, that was a disgrace.

Extra charges on the phone bill were disgraceful. So was my ragtag garden. It got to be a joke, thank heavens, and before I got as far as, "It's a dis . . . ," Debby and I were laughing. I sometimes laughed all by myself just thinking what I hadn't said aloud.

Martina Navratilova is in a television ad about buying a Subaru, and the tag line is "What do we know about it; we're just girls." Historically speaking, all of us "girls" have always known that we are supposed to be an easy mark. But, of course, we aren't. Never have been. Never will be, at twenty-one or eighty-one.

Bob wanted me to negotiate the last deal for my own car, using all my aging-feminist strengths to get as decent a price as he might have. "Don't dizzy me around," this proverbial little old lady in tennis shoes told Ricart (the biggest dealership in the world) and they didn't. In truth, they are not hard to do business with, but they let me think that I was in the driver's seat, to coin a phrase. I even told them that I would only lease the car if they gave me a cell phone and had it installed. They did and I did. So why should it be such a problem to end a lease when the owner has died? Ask GM. Getting rid of a new Cadillac should not be so hard to do. It was less than a year old, with only three hundred miles on it. Bob had leased his car in April and by September was too sick to drive. Cadillac was adamant that the car was ours for the life of the lease, not for the life of my husband. And because getting out of the remaining lease was impossible, the beautiful dark green, white-topped, too-big-for-me car sat in our garage. Finally, the lease ran out on my just-right-size car and I had a decision to make. Should I drive Bob's car for the balance of the lease and worry about a car next April? Should I be extravagant and get myself a car now that I would enjoy, or should I drive the tank, beautiful, shiny, and new but, nevertheless, a tank? There must be worse things in the world of transportation than navigating the City Center parking garage with a wheel-base the length of an elephant, so I chose to give the Cadillac a whirl. Well, not whirl exactly.

In the scheme of things aggravating, getting back my own license plates to put on Bob's car only entailed three phone calls and two letters. Comparatively, it was a slam dunk. I left my Chrysler at the dealership and came home to have Debby put my plates on Bob's car and to call the cell-phone company and cancel my contract. The phone was mounted in my car and it would have cost more to take it out, move it to the Cadillac, and then take it out again next April. I simply wanted to give up that phone. "I cannot disconnect that number," I was told, "unless Mr. Greene authorizes it himself." "That is not possible," I explained. "Then we must see the death certificate," I was told. The Chrysler with the phone is sitting in an open lot at the dealership, available to one and all. The way my world is turning these days, one and all will use it to call Azerbaijan. So I decide to hand deliver the death certificate, my maiden voyage in the Cadillac, and, of course, the battery is dead. I call AAA, who come immediately; they jump-start it, and follow me to the gas station because there are only fumes left in the gas tank and I am afraid of running out of gas before I have crept the two blocks to the Shell station. After I pump it $22 worth of gas and start the motor, it dies again. That little two-block drive wasn't enough to allow the battery to hold a charge. Nice AAA is still at the gas station and they jump-start it again. I come home, call Debby (the car with the motor running in the driveway), pick her up, and off we go to Airtouch Cellular, where she sits in the don't-dare-turn-off-the-motor car and I go inside and present the death certificate. It is all such a useless performance, but it doesn't make me sad; it makes me furious. I am getting back some of my self-sufficiency and I am ready to take on the world, at least my little suburban, Midwest corner of it. But doesn't the whole mess seem like a disgrace?

PhyllisandBob

$\mathcal{A}$LL THE ADVICE to authors I have ever read has been: write what you know about, and lordy, lordy, do I now know about being a widow.

I always have and always will think of myself as PhyllisandBob. We have a painting that Debby did for Bob's seventieth birthday, that she carried from California to Florida. It is a portrait of us against a background that says "Phyllis loves Bob loves Phyllis loves Bob loves Phyllis loves Bob," over and over again. Indeed, we did. Just as our names so comfortably sound like one person, so did our very being. We were so much of a mind that, from another room, I could ask or comment or suggest almost anything on any subject, and Bob would have been thinking of the same thing. It was a phenomenon because it happened so often without a common reminder that might have led us to the subject.

So now, whether I believe in the hereafter or not, whether I think (or just hope) that Bob is watching over me, or checking up on me, or whether it is respect for his memory, I find myself doing things that are not mine, but his. Like having the car washed. I don't do any back roads driving, and even if I did, a little dirt has never hurt anyone. But now that I am driving his car, which he chose so carefully for its color, for its top, for its tires, I am at the car wash every other week. I went for the ultra-special, extra-deluxe $12.99 deal yesterday, even though I knew that the first rainfall in months was predicted for today. And oil changes have always been below my radar screen. My in-town driving is minimal, and it takes more than three months for three thousand miles to roll that odometer. With this Cadillac, though, you just cannot ignore oil changes. By the time three months had elapsed, the car was just sitting in the garage. By the time I began to drive it, a year had passed. So each time I would turn on the motor, a flashing light said over and over, TIME TO CHANGE YOUR OIL, TIME TO CHANGE YOUR OIL. Ordered around by a car, I meekly took it to Speedy-Lube and did as I was told. I don't know whether Bob would have been ticked at the senseless expenditure, or glad that I was so conscientious about mainte-nance.

Old habits die hard, even your husband's. The espaliered tree that almost always fails to neatly espalier on the front of our house, for all these years could have drooped over the front walk and I wouldn't have noticed. But Bob noticed and clipped it back with abandon. This summer I, too, wield a mean clippers.

What's more, I, on occasion, have done something that would have made him nervous, but, when I do, I acknowledge it to one and all. Last January, when it was dark by five o'clock, I needed to have my hair cut and the only appointment I could get was 5:30. This was just a month after Bob's death and I was still adhering 100 percent to the old guidelines. Home before dark was the way Bob felt I would be safe.

Even in the years when I did a lot of volunteer work, I would, at meetings, at dusk, close my notebook, powder my nose, and start for home. I may not always have been there for the final adjournment, but Bob was spared any worry about my well-being. And so, as I walked into the beauty parlor, I told not only Mary, who has been doing my hair for years, but anyone within earshot: This is the first thing I have done that Bob would not have wanted me to do. Meaning, "Bob, wherever you are, I will be careful. Please don't worry."

Doing things the careful way likely explains the ritual I go through every night. When I am not going out, I carefully check the outside doors, the Malibu lights, the garage door and I am settled in. On nights when I am going out, first thing I do is put my house keys in my purse. Then on to a preset lighting pattern: outside lights, kitchen, living room, sitting room, and, lastly, my bedroom. Then I turn back my bed so that everything will be ready for me when I come home. It's what I did as a wife. I am still the Phyllis of PhyllisandBob.

A Date That Will Live . . .

*T*HE DAY THAT I found out that the journal could be expanded into a book was November 7, the day that would have been my fifty-eighth anniversary. Coincidences have continually intrigued me, but now they suggest, in this more sophisticated world, a certain spiritual look at life, a message of synchronicity that explains our relationship to each other.

What a coincidence, what a synchronism that I should be beginning another long-term relationship, with my computer, with my project, with my future on this date. Searching HistoryChannel.com, I found little to be historically memorable about

November 7: in 1637, Anne Hutchinson was banished from the Massachusetts Bay Colony for heresy; in 1867, Nobel Prize–winning physicist Marie Curie was born; and in 1918, news of the end of World War I sent the New York Stock Exchange into a premature state of jubilation. On November 7, 1942, Generals Eisenhower and Montgomery were preparing to give chase to General Rommel and to start the African campaign, and Bob and I were married.

The first draft, pre–World War II, called Bob to service. He left for Camp Shelby in Mississippi on January 28, 1941. He was to be out in a year. I was at college and had no part in taking him to Fort Hayes in Columbus for induction, or seeing him off at Union Station. We corresponded during those months into the spring of '41; I was studying for the General Exam, a monster, two-day test that, if I failed, would keep me from graduating from Wellesley. He was running the motor pool and going through the Louisiana maneuvers. We were good friends, not yet in love.

He had a two-week leave early in June and we saw each other daily. By the time he went back to Camp

Shelby in Hattiesburg, Mississippi, we knew that we belonged together.

And then it was December 7 and Pearl Harbor. No draftee was getting out of the service. This country was in it for the long haul. Bob applied to and was accepted as a member of the twenty-eighth class of the Infantry Officers' Training School, and left in April for Fort Benning to become a "ninety-day wonder," an officer. He had always been a gentleman.

It was impossible to convince my parents that we should be allowed to become engaged. They liked him fine, but they did not like my marrying a newly minted second lieutenant, infantry, practically on his way overseas. For months, we were as determined as the Allied forces and just as strategic in our planning, and finally achieved our goal: We announced our engagement in July; we would be married in November.

After four long months of preparing a trousseau for Medford, Oregon (!), including lingerie hand-made by nuns of the Carmelite Order, my mother was satisfied that I was now ready to embark on this unknown journey called wedlock. We went by train to Portland: my mother, Bob's mother, and I. No planes then for civilian travel, and not too many train berths. I slept most of the way across the country. The mothers played endless games of gin.

Somehow we managed reservations at the Hotel Benson, flowers and a photographer had been arranged for, a Rabbi had been contacted, and Lois and Harry, our intimate and dear Columbus friends, came from Seattle, where the FBI had assigned Harry. For Lois and me, it was a third-generation relationship: our grandfathers had been business partners, their children (our mothers) had been friends since girlhood, and Lois and I grew up across the street from one another. Plus, our fathers were first cousins. And, for Bob, when Harry arrived from Norfolk, he definitely "spoke the language," but with a deep southern drawl that he never lost—and so the future husbands also became best friends.

We became two couples joined at the hip: if one of us was invited to a party, so was the other; if a gift needed to be sent, we sent it together. It was a fortuitous synchronism that had put us all on the West Coast so that they could be our matron of honor and best man.

It was wonderful. In the preceding few months,

when Bob had arrived in Oregon with the cadre of the 91st Division, he had been dispatched to Portland to interview Clark Burguard, a Medal of Honor winner from the 91st Division of World War I. Of course, Clark was taken with Bob. He invited him to use the Multnomah Athletic Club and offered him the use of a car for the wedding weekend. Thus we invited Clark and his father to our wedding service and a lovely dinner in a private dining room of the hotel. Two very nice strangers, the only real guests. I didn't feel cheated at all not to have a bridal gown and veil or a gaggle of bridesmaids. My light blue not-quite-silk dress was fine; Bob was in uniform. His $166.66 a month (and "that's every month," Bob always laughingly said) would support us, and thus we became Second Lieutenant and Mrs. Robert B. Greene.

We were lucky enough to have two plane tickets to San Francisco. My mother gave us the liquor left from the wedding dinner, some had been opened, some had not. We couldn't fit it into Bob's valpak but I had room in my luggage and off we flew into the night, in a DC-9. By 2:00 A.M., we were at the St. Francis Hotel—where they had not saved our room. Kindly, very kindly, they gave us the bridal suite for the night. That night, only, believe me. We opened my luggage to find a wet mess of clothes, sodden with scotch. In a nonpressurized baggage compartment, the corks had come out of the half-used bottles. Carefully packed in navy blue monogrammed lingerie bags, the handmade wedding nightgown had huge purpley patches from the blue dye. So did everything else, including the wedding dress. We draped it all around the living room of the suite, which now smelled like a distillery. I suppose we had a choice about our reaction, but it just seemed the most natural thing in the world to throw up our hands, helplessly, and laugh. It was a completely unconscious setting of criteria for the best way to live our lives. Not that we always managed to.

I still sometimes think, after all these years, of the beautiful turquoise velvet robe that I left in San Francisco, where, if you are to believe Tony Bennett, you are only supposed to lose your heart. That, I had already done.

Lefty Loosey,
Righty Tighty

HERE IS MORE to keeping a house than housekeeping. So far, in my solo mission, I have had to buy a new garage door opener and a complete new air-conditioner unit. With the air conditioner, I got a service warranty, but none for the existing furnace. So I made a note on my calendar to get one come fall. Still, I was beset by maintenance questions. Will I be able to reset the automatic thermostat? Who do I call for the sliding glass door to the deck that has become impossible to move? I think to look in Bob's desk and there! there! is a file marked "Appliance, service, roofing, trees, *etc.*" and in it are old paid bills, receipts, telephone numbers, everything and everyone the keeper of a house needs to know. All of the service people who I have had to call remember Bob, and are helpful to me. It is a gift in a file. It beats the Yellow Pages hands down.

Today they came to close the pool. What a relief. It has been an aggravation (and an expense) all summer long. At first I thought I would be able to add the bromine to the brominator myself. One of the last things Bob was able to physically do was hobble down the flagstones—treacherous, treacherous—and show me how to do it. And then Rusty from Quality Pool showed me again this spring. And I wrote it all down (of course), and kept my notes on top of the bromine tub. The first time I tried to do it, I was just too slow, and too inept, to get the top back on the brominator in time and I lost my prime. With this pool, getting the prime back is a major endeavor. The water has to flow uphill, which water just doesn't do.

I gave up and called Quality for weekly service, but they were already overcommitted in this time of labor shortages. Good for the economy, bad for me. So I tried another company whose crotchety owner had also become their service man, in this time of labor shortages. Good for the economy, even worse for me this time around. Never have I been treated so rudely and contemptuously, barking at any small request I might make, wheezing with his emphysema while lighting yet another cigarette. And the pool stayed cloudy.

Toward the end of the summer I called Quality again and, in Bob's name, I beseeched them to *help! help!*, which they did, and now this summer of pool misery is over. If it was used ten times, that's a lot.

Building our pool was one of the biggest thrills of Bob's life, and what he enjoyed was not only the floating around, and the entertaining around, but the working around. He skimmed the leaves and he tested the chemicals and he used all the equipment to keep it in shape for more than twenty-five years.

At last, the towels have been retrieved from the pool house and washed, the floats are stored for the winter. Soon, if I am lucky, I will find someone to put the outdoor furniture away and I can turn my eyes toward the season ahead. This is the season I have not been through alone, and this, I think, is the hardest season of all.

There's a lot more to learn about maintaining a house than securing a pool service or calling the plumber or electrician or gardener. That is often the necessary way of doing things, and I envy the do-it-yourselfers although I would rather see than be one. Still and all, for a reasonably healthy octogenarian, there are some chores that you truly need to manage for yourself, like watering the grass. I know how to turn on a spigot, but coordinating two spigots at once is confusing. If the garage spigot is turned to the left (*lefty loosey*, in case "on" and "off" are difficult to grasp—well, they are for me), then the outdoor spigot needs to remain *righty tighty* until you are out of the reach of the spray. It actually takes advance planning in this house to water the lawn on the east side. From the yard side, to the garage, to the yard side, to the garage . . . finally, the "ons" are in sync and you are safely out of harm's (the water's) way. It sounds so idiotic to write about it, but all summer long it was a big deal and a big problem.

It's getting so that doing anything efficiently seems to be beyond my capabilities. And I know it isn't age, it has to do with being alone. Why else do I buy gas and forget to put the cap back on before I drive away? Why can't I get the trunk to lock on the car when I close it? There's a trick that I *know* (Bob showed me often enough) to just touch it down, not slam it, but today I tried six or eight times in the Kroger's parking lot until some sympathetic man came over to my car and did it for me. Physical limitations I will accept; mental lapses are just the same old senior moments that we all have, but why am I turning into a helpless woman? If helping myself is beginning to be a lost art, I'd better enroll in a how-to course and learn it again.

Sleep (and) Disorder

THERE IS A HOUSE across the little ravine in the backyard. Our neighbors have lived there for almost ten years, and although we have been cordial to each other—they once invited us to a fund-raiser they were hosting; Bob once called them in the middle of the night because he saw a fire by their back door—our paths haven't really crossed. About four months after Bob died, the neighbor wife died. We didn't know each other well enough to attend each other's funerals; we didn't even send notes. But now, at 3:00 A.M., as I look across the little valley separating us, the poignancy of the situation hits me full force. We may be almost strangers. We have not had enough in common to generate a friendship. I would not even know the man if I saw him. But that light in his bedroom late at night tells me all I need to know about him. I know his heart.

When I lie down to go to sleep, I tell myself: "Don't think." I did it when Bob was sick and I do it now. It doesn't always work, but when it does, I accept it as a blessing. Whoever would have thought that closing down your mind was a good thing to do? Or that it could be interpreted as the Art of Positive Thinking: You are positively refusing to let your worries get you down. Or is it just another way of being in denial? Psychobabble aside, believe Frank Sinatra's oft-repeated phrase, "Whatever gets you through the night."

Last night I awoke at 3:00 A.M., a habit I would like to break. I grabbed something to read. As a rule, reading in bed is my favorite pastime, but at that dreary and lonely hour, it is not usually rewarding. Last night I picked up *The New Yorker* to read a review of a new biography of Vince Lombardi. That is not as far-fetched as it sounds; I do like pro football and I did cheer on the Green Bay Packers. What made me sit up in bed and say "oh" aloud, however, was when I came to a passage about Lombardi teaching his sweep to "an audience of wide-eyed coaches for eight hours . . . chief among the men listening was Sid Gillman, about to become the coach of the San Diego Chargers. Gillman, who will never be the subject of a biography, is by far the most influential coach of the last forty years." The article goes on to explain how Gillman understood that you could use the passing game in the same way that Lombardi used the running game.

What memories his name evoked. In those long-ago, innocent days, it was standard procedure for men with money and position to help poor but athletic young men come to the The Ohio State University, find jobs for them, and underwrite their tuition. In those long-ago and innocent days, these athletes really worked at jobs and graduated with authentic degrees in business or dentistry or accounting. Football was the holy grail at Ohio State, and Sid was an athlete sponsored by friends of my parents. I had a mind-altering crush on him. He and I were once at the same dinner table, and after dinner, he went in the yard with all of us kids and we tossed a football around! Be still my heart! Another time, at a party after my confirmation, he danced a few steps with me. Would he even remember my name now? I don't think so. But finding his name in the middle of the night gave me a chance to remember who I once was, with what joy and hope the adolescent-me looked forward to the life ahead. Even then I knew it wouldn't be this actual Sid Gillman who would fulfill my dreams, but I was sure there would be someone out there in the world for me. And at 3:00 A.M., I could look back and see that my knight in shining armor had ridden into town in a heavily financed yellow convertible that he called "the flying omelet," that the happy years that followed had been duplicated by thousands and thousands of other lucky couples of my generation, "the greatest generation," and I put the magazine down and went to sleep.

Talking to other widows, I find that each has her own way: listen to the radio, or read, or take a pill. I have yet to talk to anyone who just sleeps soundly through the night. In the morning, if a child or a friend calls to ask how are you, the answer is always, "I'm okay" or "fine" or however you choose to define your state of being. You hardly ever say sleepless; it has become an ordinary fact of life.

Killing Time, or Using It

*A*LL OF MY LIFE I have had my nose in a book. If I don't have one going, I feel as if a part of me is missing. It didn't always please Bob to know how high a priority I put on reading, but he was a reader, too, though not as compulsive as I, and he understood, just like he understood everything else about me.

It can be 3:00 A.M. when a book can be a sedative, or 3:00 P.M. when a book is an information resource, or 9:00 P.M. when a book becomes sheer pleasure in your hands, but, for me, books have always been the all-purpose restorative.

Others instinctively pick up knitting, or quilting,

or cross-stitching, or a deck of cards or turn on the radio or do a crossword puzzle. When you live alone, the activities we are talking about here are essentials.

Bob used to say, so often, come midafternoon, "Another wasted day," because we had really done nothing much but talk to each other, turn the TV to CNBC, half-watching the ticker-tape symbols, maybe go on an errand or two. Seemingly squandered hours at the time were, in remembrance, precious, and I think we both actually knew it. Having the company of your husband, if only to watch TV together, or sit companionably reading different books, or doing the crossword puzzle—what a gift that was. Having always been motivated to be doing *something*, even a leisure-time activity counts; it is impossible to do *nothing*. Perhaps, in your wife-life, TV counted as doing nothing much of the time. When you are alone, even just the noise of the TV, another voice in the house, is pleasant. There are times that I cannot believe that I am watching a cooking show (not that I can't use the instruction) and I begin to think that maybe becoming a real cook would be more constructive than passively sitting and watching someone else do it on TV. There are always friends (and if you are of a certain age, there are always ailing friends) who would appreciate a treat or a meal. Plus, you have to shop for the food, deliver the food gift, and so you do something for others while you have the satisfaction of being the doer.

If we watch too much TV, we are all afraid of being perceived as the soap-opera-watching stereotype, lying on the couch eating bonbons. Actually, if that is what we have the time to do and that is what we want to do, we should. I have stood by CBS and Walter Cronkite and Dan Rather since the beginning of time. If Saturday night is the loneliest night of the week, then Sunday, now, is a day and a half. But in the morning, I have "Sam and Cokie" and in the evening "60 Minutes."

For women too young for Medicare and Social Security and pensions and retirement, these waste-of-time worries seem frivolous. In the face of concerns about rearing children alone and providing for them and for your own well-being, they hardly seem worth considering. When you are half as old, it is twice as bad. Losing a young husband is a tragedy; no one can quite call it tragedy when you are both in your seventies or eighties. But alone is alone, at thirty or eighty.

I remember being at a very big and noisy cocktail party in a lovely home with a lively crowd. I was nowhere near the door to the living room when I saw a young widow walk in, pause, look around, stand for a few minutes, then turn and leave. The host and hostess would never have let this happen, but they were lost in the milling mass and never saw her arrive. At the time, for me, it was a small, sad incident. I wished I could have caught her eye and greeted her. Now that I have experienced going to a big party unescorted, I know that there is no such thing as sad and small. When it is happening to you, it is sad and huge.

When, in 1907, Franz Lehar wrote *The Merry Widow*, he didn't know what he was talking about. There just ain't no such.

Along with Bob's "wasted day" line was another he often used. After breakfast, he would say, "Well, I have to do my work," and he would do the daily crossword puzzle.

Not the hard *New York Times*, just the *Columbus Dispatch*. I find myself, now, doing that work, too. Am I killing time or using my mind, even that little bit, to keep the vocabulary juices flowing? Whichever it is, it is what this widow does. And I hear my friends say they do the same, as if admitting to a small crime.

If sitting idle is the devil's handiwork, remember these are devilish times, and it is your prerogative to occupy yourself in any way that is helpful to you. The habits of a lifetime do return, and we all seem to return to the "real" world, changed but still the same in many ways. If I ever have my portrait painted (which, of course, I won't), I would choose to pose with a book on my lap. But then I'd have to have my glasses on.

Doing Well =
Doing Good

*T*HERE WAS AN ARTICLE in the *Orange County Register* about Betty Baker, who founded a group called Special Friends for older, single lonely women who want company with whom they can go to the movies or share a meal or play bridge or sit together and knit. Starting the club was just another activity for Betty, who fills her life with things to do; she also serves as an usher at the Performing Arts Center or South Coast Repertory, and as a guide at the Anaheim Convention Bureau. There are opportunities aplenty, and organizations that can fit those opportunities to your skills and interests. We need to be busy, and all the better if by helping others we reap some benefits, too.

Volunteerism has long been my cause. The health of the community, its organizations and hospitals and fund-raising activities depend on citizens who freely give their time and talent. Companies that offer their employees release time to work in schools or for the United Way or on boards and projects are offering real support, much more than dollars alone can do. I am proud to have played a role in establishing the Information and Referral Center, which has grown into a major agency called FirstLink, a connection center between those who have and those who need. Their major purpose is to link those people needing the help of the social service agencies with the most appropriate help available. When it first began, one of our goals was to allow a client to call I and R and, on the same dime, be connected to the people who could help them. No one has profited more from the advances in technology than this agency in being able to meet its goals.

When Robert Taft was elected governor of Ohio in 1998, he and his wife, Hope, began promoting a program called Ohio Reads, encouraging people to volunteer in the schools; it sounded like something I would enjoy doing, and I went for my training to

FirstLink. I have been at this long enough to remember that there was a time when the school administration was very reluctant to have citizens inside their building because they wanted to conceal their own inadequacies. Now they are eager for help (oh, do they need help) and these volunteers, after training by FirstLink in tandem with Big Brothers–Big Sisters and a police check, are welcomed with open arms. I was assigned a school in my own neighborhood and a fourth grader, a happy, friendly, giggling eleven-year-old for whom Ohio Reads was invented. I was to go at lunch hour; we would eat together, and then tackle her assignments. Too much for a short time, but a way to begin. I packed my lunch, enough for the two of us, and she picked hers up in the cafeteria line. She ate nothing of hers (I couldn't blame her), but she didn't want any of what I had brought either. Not egg salad sandwiches, or peanut butter and jelly, or chips or brownies. In the two weeks we were together before I had my surprise heart problems and ended up in the hospital, I felt as if we had been establishing something of a small relationship, and I hated the imposed hiatus. I hope to go back soon.

You can read to the blind, you can translate books into braille, your church or synagogue may ask you to visit the sick in hospitals (although my personal bias in the hospital is to be left alone. I'm not even particularly cordial to those nice "pink ladies" who bring the menus around). I remember, from helping establish the Volunteer Action Center, that what the nurses used to dread most was to have doctors' wives volunteer on their floor. Beware the snitch.

The next best thing to being with your own grandchild is to be a foster grandparent, teamed up with a nursery school. Or take a pet from the humane society to either the nursery school or the nursing home. If there isn't a ready-made volunteer job, you can invent one, like Betty Baker and her Special Friends. Or, if you are adept with the computer, you can teach others and open up a whole, new exciting world.

These are all things that work. That is why you have read them so many times before, yet why I felt they needed to be included here.

The Tao and
the Dow

THERE IS A BEAUTIFUL BOOK, *The Hours*, by Michael Cunningham, that won the Pulitzer Prize. It was inspired by Virginia Woolf's *Mrs. Dalloway*, and until I had seen the new video with Vanessa Redgrave, the book was confusing to me. But once I was oriented about who was who, I immersed myself in the characters and the magnificent writing and similes. The end, though, did me in. Richard, the obscure but prize-winning poet is ready to give up—sick with AIDS, alone, living in messy poverty. He is about to win a prize of some sort, after which his longtime friend Clarissa is throwing a party for him, yet he, like Hamlet, centuries before, has found the world

"Tomorrow, tomorrow and tomorrow, weary, stale, flat and unprofitable," and he says, "But there are still the hours, aren't there? One and then another, and you get through that one and then, my God, there's another."

At my most bereft, I feel these hours of aloneness exquisitely, painfully. Most of the time, there is this consolation, says Cunningham, "an hour here or there when our lives seem, against all odds and expectations, to burst open and give us everything we've ever imagined. . . ." It is because I have had those hours, too, that my down days are fewer than my up.

I can remember exactly one such hour that was perfect, and I knew it as it was happening. We had gone to Maine to visit Tim at camp. We had spent the day there, reveling in his high-jumping ability. He was such a little kid at twelve, but he could do four feet seven, and all of the visitors, not just the proud parents, were ooh-ing and aah-ing. We had come back to the expensive (beyond our means), rickety-chic resort where we were staying with friends. Bob had poured me a drink and I stood on the steps of the slightly musty cabin that we had rented that was considered the *in* cabin (*in* less need of refurbishing than the others?).

I smelled the pine smell, and felt Lake Kezar nearby. I had had a happy, upbeat letter from Bobby and Debby, who had not come on this trip. I remember that Bobby had closed his note by saying that he had to finish because the waitress had just brought him a glass of champagne—a big joke from a high school senior who was feeling lucky to have been left home without a baby-sitter! I almost felt overwhelmed by that sense of complete joy, of that perfect moment, of God being in his heaven and all being right in the world.

Many years later, on January 28, 1997, we were sitting on the beach on Longboat Key, and I took out a small piece of paper that I had in my beach bag and I wrote:

So this is what it comes to for a happy marriage: a perfect morning on a beautiful beach, in compatibility, contentment, and love, knowing without sorrow that the best has been and is not, as the poet said, yet to be; secure (reasonably) that the children, though not completely problem free, are better established than many, and that the grand-children can see golden promises ahead. My father died fifty-nine years ago today. He was 52.

I carried that little scrap of paper in my wallet until I began my journal on December 31, 1998, and then I pasted it inside the front cover.

In December 1999, Debby gave me *365 Tao*, daily meditations that shed a Taoist light on every facet of life. Only because she asked me to, I started reading it nightly, about aging and being and bravery and friendship and joy. I'm not that fast a religious study, but it didn't take me long to see that she had given me another guide to inner tranquillity and the recog-nition (rerecognized, I guess) that all religion leads to the same place of grace. One day on the phone she mentioned something that she thought I would be pleased about in the Dow, and I broke in to ask, "The Dow? The Dow is down 265 points!" I had not realized that these meditations had been written by Deng-Ming-Dao, nor would I have known Tao was pronounced Dow. So in the utterly goofy conversa-tion that followed, until we figured out that one man's Tao is another's Dow, we had a great laugh. A fringe benefit.

When the children were in elementary school, sometimes, when a reliable sitter could be found, we would go over to Main Street, to Kuennings, a landmark Columbus restaurant that had moved from downtown to our suburb. It became a place for us to have a low-key night out, a drink and dinner in the paneled bar, our neighborhood watering hole. Our "Cheers" when Ted Danson was still a kid.

One night we happened to be sitting near neighbors from the next street over, Bud and Did, whose son Davo often walked to school with our daughter, Debby. Why Bud and I began to talk about life's blessings, I cannot fathom. It was an unlikely subject for that time and that place. But what Bud told me that evening I have never forgotten. He said that every morning when he awoke, he looked at the hinges on the doors in his bedroom and counted his blessings. Blessed to be secure and warm and comfortable, with a happy family, a successful real estate business, a loving wife. He didn't spell it all out for me that night, he just told me that there are blessings in hinges (sermons in stone and good in everything, I noted in my head).

It was an odd conversation. We were not intimate friends and this seemed a very personal thing to tell me, but how grateful I am that he did. I know when it popped into my mind again. It was on the day that Bud died, much too young, leaving that lovely house and the loving family and the hinges of happiness.

Did became a very young widow who maintained her tranquillity and her smile and her gentle demeanor as she bravely survived the death of a son-in-law in an automobile accident, the death of her brother with Alzheimer's (the brother who had named her Did because as a child he could not say Virginia), the death of her own son, and a litany of sorrows that would lay low the strongest of women.

What had sustained her? Could it have been the memories that lived on in the hinges? While there have been times these last months when I thought my euphoria account had been overdrawn, I still have hinges and blessings and rare moments when my life seems to burst open and give me everything.

With a Little Help from My Friends

ONCE, MANY YEARS AGO, when my mother was in the hospital in Florida after suffering a surprise heart attack, as my brother and I were leaving after a long day in the intensive-care unit, we came upon a little woman in the hospital lobby, crying. Her husband was on dialysis, he was dying, it was pouring rain, and she couldn't get a taxi to take her to the apartment they had recently moved into from New York. My brother, being the kind of kind person that he is, offered to take her home. Where or how we went from the hospital to wherever it was she lived, I have no idea. It was an endless drive in a downpour and we never encountered her again in the halls of

St. Francis Hospital. Can you imagine how a man, who does that for a stranger, treats his widowed sister? Not only he, but my sister-in-law and their children have made me feel so well-included in holidays and festivities, with phone calls and plans, that I know I have a support system that cannot be rivaled.

There are so many others who care for me . . . take care of me . . . that I am never lonely for long. In that way, I am truly blessed, because I am one of the last leaves on the tree, one of the last living members of my crowd.

I only hope that all of you who read this have your Lois and Harry, who asked me, every night, to eat what they were eating, or go where they were going, or come down to their nearby house for a drink; your Chuck and Dotty, who take me to the nicest places and for the memories Chuck and I share as stepsiblings but, even more, lifelong friends; your Jackies and Junes, Bettys and Sukies and Ibbys and Sallys and Bobs and Bills, Libbys and Shirles and Cees and Marys and Peggys and Judys—the kind of friends we all need to get us through the days. I play mah-jongg every Monday with four women a decade younger than I. They have been so dear to me, making me lose a decade of age once a week, and when we don't play, when they are away for the winter, they will e-mail or call: Reva and Joyce and Pat and Hilda and Joanie. When our own ranks of contemporaries thin, there are good, compatible people out in the world waiting to offer their friendship. And because I was lucky enough to be involved in this community, that's another bank of affection into which I can and do tap, as well as old, old high school friends: Char and Marcia and Carolyn, and long-distance friends who can and do call, day and night, now that all those competitive companies keep slashing prices to get our business. College friends stay in touch, so Jean and Alice and I pick up as if the Class of '41 were still in session. Florida friends from all those years we vacationed together: Joan and Nancy and Hope and Betty, not only reminiscing but talking books and travel. These little pockets of goodwill are available to all of us. Often, we need to make the effort and initiate contact. Sitting home alone, even with a book or knitting or cooking for company, is just not fulfilling enough.

Bob and I were still leading the good life of a retired couple, together in our very own house, in our very own community when, in 1995, I think, my daughter sent me an article from a Los Angeles paper about a woman whose husband, a General Motors executive, had retired, and they had moved to a new community. She missed her old home, her old friends, and she had yet to make new ones. But she found them right at her fingertips, on the screen in front of her. This glimpse of another world looked exciting to me, who knew little of the Internet or America Online. I bought a Mac and began the search for cyberfriends, and there they were, right on the screen, in Seniornet, in the Book Discussion and Review forum. Since the day I found this group, I have posted a message almost daily and I have read the many messages that appear there.

The names of my friends are e-mail names: Shirlsbt and Garvin and Traude and Gchap and Carriecan. I am WedeWede, my grandmother name, given to me by Maggie when she was very little. She started to say it to me because I called her "sweetie," and she thought that was the way we address one another. When she learned phonetic spelling, sweetie became wede, and now it is my name to nieces and their husbands and daughters-in-law and grandchildren of friends. I'm not sure where my book friends live, although when Jo in ABQ became Jo in Tx, we had a clue. I don't know if they are male or female, but when someone recently posted that the "geezers" are certainly on the move, across their towns and across the state and across the country, another answered that it's more like "geezerettes," for we are mostly older widows with a commonality that has made us cherish one another, beyond our literary preferences alone. Though faceless, these computer friends have been a godsend to me. I understand their hearts, I admire their minds, and I heed their advice. We talk mainly about books, what we are reading, what we think does not pass the hundred-page test (if you don't like it by then, you have permission not to finish), about Oprah's book club, and then we segue into the news, and even shoes, and a few cooking tips. We never "flame" another reader for choices of books or critiques. We are tolerant and respectful of each other. Let me quote from a message from Shirlsbt:

I think what makes this forum unique is the status of age and I mean that in a very positive sense. In the past four years I have learned to respect all of you, because at our age we bring a very large platter to the table. I have also learned which of you enjoy the same kind of reading that I do. Let's just continue to learn from each other, and my dear friends, share the good times and the bad.

I posted little when Bob was sick, but the few times I did, I mentioned that these were hard days for me. I know I told them that if Bob would doze off, I was reading *A Man in Full* as I sat in the room with him. Just as books always do, Tom Wolfe could transport me from that chair, surrounded by medicine bottles and scheduled dosages, to a plantation or a prison. It was well into December before I could bring myself to tell them that Bob had died. I had so many condolence messages from them, all so comforting . . . none more meaningful than this from Arlvh:

> I lost my mother while serving on the board of our local housing authority and one of our tenants asked me if I was suffering "happy grief" or "bitter grief." Happy grief, she explained is when you are at peace with the separation even tho it is causing

you pain. Bitter grief is when something is left undone that you will never be able to finish, words that you wish you had spoken but never will. I really have shortened her explanation a great deal but I know you understand what I mean. I know that your grief is "happy grief." You are in my prayers and the prayers of all of our friends here. If there is anything we can do to make it easier for you, we will.

They have done much for me by sharing their reading lists and their insights and, yes, their long-distance love.

Very recently they chose my son Bob's book *Duty: A Father, His Son and the Man Who Won the War* as a monthly reading selection and, by now, they know that Wedewede and I are one and the same person.

There are new friends, too. Strangers one minute, friends the next. Just last week I went into TJ Maxx to buy a few pair of knee-high hose to wear under pant suits. And I asked idly if they sold handkerchiefs. Women's handkerchiefs seem to have gone out of fashion with the buggy whip. I guess you are supposed to keep Kleenex in your purse, but old-fashioned though it may be, it's the old-fashioned hankie I crave. To own one is to lose one, of course, and all the beautifully monogrammed and delicate handkerchiefs that my mother brought from Europe are strewn in every restaurant and store and volunteer meeting room in the city. The woman I asked said they did not sell them nor, I knew, do the department stores. Lord knows, I've looked. "But," said this salesperson, "I have a box that someone gave me as a gift, still wrapped, and I don't use them. I'll be glad to give them to you. I was just going to throw them in the bag that I'm taking to the Cancer Ray thrift shop." I offered to pay for them but she wouldn't hear of it. All I needed do was come in the next day and she would bring them to work. Which I did and she did. So I promised myself that I will do an unexpected kindness to a stranger as soon as I can. Thus is goodness passed on in a world so often sadly lacking in civility.

That was just my good intention as I left the store and, suddenly, this is a theme that has been reaffirmed by a snowballing movement that promotes "paying forward." As a philosophy, it is old hat in

Columbus. Woody Hayes, the legendary coach, preached that message all the time, not only to his players but to anyone who would listen. And that was a lot of people.

In 1993 a Bakersfield college business professor, tired of hearing about the many "random acts of violence," had his class go out and "commit random acts of kindness." Oprah Winfrey heard of this blind Professor Wall and invited him to be on her show. What had been for many years a way of life for good and decent people, now assumed the aura of a cult. Catherine Ryan Hyde wrote a novel, *Pay It Forward*, which I had read and enjoyed last summer. Now there is a movie, based on the book, and there are lapel pins and T-shirts and a website. There is the Pay It Forward Foundation and the Random Acts of Kindness Foundation and Kindness, Inc.

If it is a real, maintainable movement and not just a fad, widows might be among the first to reap the rewards.

To Market, to Market

*I*N THE OLD NURSERY RHYME, we went to market, to market, to buy a fat pig. How many trips have I made, home again, home again, jiggedy-jig with not only the fat pig but with bags and bags of food: the unhealthy Hostess snowballs, both the pink and the white, packed side by side with the meat and potatoes and vegetables. Food meaning family, food meaning all kinds of sustenance, food as love.

Those trips to the grocery were so frequent and so automatic, that I didn't even notice that it was something that I did practically daily (sometimes even twice in a day!). In fact, going to Kroger's on Main

Street was often a social outing, for it was a meeting place where friends exchanged news, discussed community issues at the meat counter, and made some decisions for organizations of common interest to many of us before we even checked out.

Today, if I go to the store once every two weeks, that is enough. I always wonder what the butcher can be thinking when I ask him to take a beef tenderloin filet and cut it horizontally, and then package the two halves separately. I know what I am thinking: two dinners, two open-face steak sandwiches, is there applesauce in the refrigerator? The salad bar, a great merchandising tool, was probably not developed with widows in mind; it is, nevertheless, a perfect way to buy just the right amount of cauliflower or broccoli or diced celery to serve the needs of one diner. I'm sure the reason for in-store caterers, who make excellent "to go" meals, was to accommodate the busy, young professionals. We senior widows reap the benefits, not because we are too busy to cook, but because we are too disinterested to cook. And never underestimate the gourmet delights of the freezer case; single-serving dinners from Healthy

Choice can make you feel virtuous for their few calories as much as for their ease of preparation. My personal favorite is Uncle Ben's frozen rice bowls. Take them from your freezer, put them in your microwave for five minutes, shovel them down in five minutes more, and there isn't even a dish to wash.

I have a friend who told me that the first time her widowed mother went to the grocery after her husband's death, she burst into tears as she picked up one baking potato to put in her cart. One potato in a grocery cart. The perfect symbol of widowhood.

From the early days of my life, when five of us would sit at the dinner table together, each in a pre-ordained place, with that dinner of meat, potatoes, vegetable, salad, and dessert, until now, when a bowl of soup and a sandwich is more than enough . . . that is a very common story that tells it all. The diminishing of a woman, the running down of a life. The table set for one, the TV for company . . . "I'll be seeing you in all the old familiar places."

Traveling Solo

I WENT TO VISIT out-of-town friends, a couple who had vacationed in the same spot we had for fourteen years. They are very dear to me; they were very dear to Bob, and Wayne and Bob spent many hours sitting in the sun, laughing and talking and revealing their true selves to each other. I wondered how I would react, going alone to visit them, to meet their "city" friends, by myself. More to their credit than mine, I think, it was a most wonderful weekend. When I wrote them a note of thanks, it was not only for the "great, good time—excellent food, excellent drink, excellent company . . . but even more than that(!), there is more, I began to recover myself as a person capable of being a *whole* person."

I have known since December 1998 that I am a single entity. As well as I have been functioning, I wasn't aware that I could pull off a series of social encounters in a strange environment, with no one to catch my eye across the table, no one to reinforce my small talk with a smile, no one to make me feel protected out in the wide world.

I have wondered, often, if I don't refer to Bob too much when I am out with friends. So many times, a funny remark he had made, or his take on a certain topic seems so apropos, that I often interpose "Bob always said" or "Remember when Bob . . ." On reflection, I realize that could make people a little uncomfortable. Maybe not now, after all these months, but surely at first. Yet I think it makes me more comfortable, having him at the table or in the room.

Here, in a different city, with new faces, I functioned not only as me, the way I had always reacted and responded to others, but also even as Me, my better, stronger self that I hope is slowly growing back, deep inside.

It's not as if I hadn't ever traveled alone before. I had been to visit our children when Bob couldn't get away. I actually looked forward to cross-country trips with a good book and no interruptions. I once went to a college reunion and lost my old roommate at Logan Airport. She was to meet me at the baggage counter, which was impossible because the Boston Celtics had arrived at the same time, with yet another NBA win to celebrate. I stayed at the airport until dark, and finally tracked her down at Wellesley.

Going to Chicago for three days may sound as if I think what I did was walk on the moon, yet for me it was a giant step for widowhood, and today I feel a lot better about myself than I did last week before I went.

I have been a very active woman and fortunate enough to play a visible role in the community. It has happened often that over the years, someone has introduced me as Bob's wife, or Bobby or Debby or Tim's mother, and just as often, someone overhearing this has said, "No, she's a person in her own right." Believe it though I did, I lost some of that person when my husband died. On this weekend visit, I found some of her again.

Carmen Ohio

For fifty years (with time out for the war), we went to the Ohio State football games, ardent fans, like everyone else in Columbus. We finally had to stop in 1997; the ramps to The Box were just too much for Bob; The Box had been our destination all of that time, on B deck on the fifty-yard line. The Box was not ours, it belonged to a family with whom we have been tangentially members, and we were lucky enough to get not only these great seats but the camaraderie of the every-Saturday get-together.

Early that summer, I had written a bittersweet poem to let them know that we just would not be there the coming fall:

This is our sad admission
Next year it will seem strange
To have broken with tradition
Put the blame on Time and Change.
But the stairs are much too steep
And the incline on the ramps
Has slowed us to a creep
As our legs get muscle cramps.
The thrill of band formations,
Each game more than a game,
Great cookies, conversations
Notre Dame (1935) to Notre Dame (1995)
So thanks, friends, for the memory,
The box, the parking passes
We'll watch it on our TV
And on our aging asses.
But this please do remember
And know without a doubt
The Greenes, come next September
Aren't giving up—just giving out.

The last time we had been in the stadium was June 1998. Our son Bob was the commencement speaker, an incredible thrill for his parents. The

"Shoe" was filled with other proud families, gathered to see their progeny graduate. This was Bob's second try, having been rained out the June before. Near the end of the speech, he told the crowd of fifty thousand that we were there, in all likelihood for the last time. And he asked the crowd to give us a standing ovation. Us. And they applauded and they stood, and in all that excitement I felt such gratitude to him for this remarkable gesture to and for us, as I was simultaneously wondering what all those people could be thinking, asking themselves, "Why them?"

It was with that resonating in my memory that I walked into the stadium this year. We had, of course, not gone last year at all. Actually, by the time football season rolled around, Bob was bedridden. He didn't really care enough to watch on TV, although we did put the game on in the early fall. By late October, we didn't even try. So except for the graduation event, I had not been there since November 1996. What warmed my heart was that all the cast of characters were there, where they ought to be. Dick, making sure I was hearing his (off-key) rendition of the "Star-Spangled Banner"; Bob-the-cookie-supplier, who always passes full bags around at halftime, had especially wrapped two snicker doodles for me before he served the rest of the group; and there was my favorite seat, near Char and Mary so that we can watch and talk (and talk and talk) all at the same time. The fact that we talked continually during the game became such an integral part of the fun that, one game, I brought a typed agenda so everyone would understand the range of our conversations.

Bob had had a special shtick of his own. When he was in the office pool and had picked a number, near the end of the game, he worked out the complicated formula that could help him take the pot: if they make a field goal and we have a touch back and then we make a touchdown and they—on and on until it would all add up to his lucky number. Another small part of the tradition.

There is a line in the Ohio State alma mater, "Carmen Ohio," that says

> *while our hearts resounding thrill*
> *with joy which death alone can still*

For the many years as I have sung that touching song, I have always thought of all the others who used to be seated there . . . Uncle Si, my mother, Bob and Hattie, Frannie, Rose—and now, in my heart, I added Bob.

More Leaves Off the Tree

$\mathcal{I}$N 1999, WHEN DECEMBER was just around the corner, I came close to that major milestone: a widow for one year. I had weathered the holidays and the birthdays, my anniversary, all of the annual joys and most of the annual annoyances (including those old favorites classified as "major capital expenses"). And then, one after the other, the loss of two wonderful old friends.

First, the Tuesday luncheon group of four men had become two. For almost fifteen years, Bob had "kept the books" on a tablet sheet, recording whose turn it was to pay. The record-keeping was a joke; the rapport at that table was not. In October, our wry, gregarious, savvy, steadfast friend Bill had died. Another empty place at the table, another empty place in my heart. The day after Bill's funeral, Chuck called me and asked what I was doing Tuesday. I told him I was going to a meeting. "Oh," he said, "I have a reservation at Rigsby's that I made last week for Bill and me, and I am still going. I thought maybe you could make it." "Of course I can," I said, the meeting becoming meaningless in light of this invitation. And I went. I'm not sure, but I don't think a wife had ever made that luncheon before. As I sat in for Bob and Bill (with the other Bob, the cookie Bob, out of town), Chuck and I, just by being there, mourned the end of another era of our lives. Without saying a word of what this table for two meant, we almost pretended that our silence might negate the truth.

Then, to emphasize that I had almost made the 360-degree/365-day lap, on December third, Harry, my friend of so many years, died.

On the day before Thanksgiving I had called Lois a little after noon and learned that Harry had been sick in the night and they were on their way to the emergency room. I went over to Mt. Carmel to sit with them until they were called in to see a doctor. Once there, Harry jokingly said to Lois, "Ask Phyllis to come back. I think we could use a third opinion," but I stayed where I was, of course, and then, in an instant, Harry lost it all and went comatose. By then, our family doctor, who we know well enough to call by his first name, had been beeped, saw Harry, and came back to the "quiet room" where they had put Lois and said: "It doesn't look good."

Harry was put on a breathing machine long enough to have gallbladder surgery, and then he lingered in the intensive care unit for three days, and died. The three days was a parade of specialists and technicians, all assorted medical personnel, changing from one day to the next.

Not too long ago there was a report in the *Journal of the American Medical Association* headlined "Medical textbooks offer little on end-of-life care." They found that the least well covered topics were social, spiritual, and family issues. Families whose primary caregiver is truly a caregiver should be grateful. Yet when unknown specialists of all kinds come to bring their expertise during the last days, there is a rude awakening with the sterile, impersonal (non)relationship. Maybe if textbooks gave more guidance to doctors-in-training about end-of-life care, more physicians would be more empathetic at this most crucial of times.

This was not just another leaf falling off the tree; it is not even a leaf off the same branch, but off the same twig. Harry's funeral was a celebration of his life, with his sons recounting his many clever quips and comments. It was the first funeral service to which I have ever been where those gathered applauded the ceremony. In fact, Lois labeled the tape made for relatives who couldn't come for the funeral "You Can't Just Bury Harry." That would have been the kind of title he would have thought up himself.

So now, reliving the first bad months following December 1998, I think there should have been a way to help Lois through her first blast of widowhood in December 1999. Having been down the widow's walk, did I help show her a path? I don't know.

All in the Same Boat

*I*T WAS ALMOST startling to me to have had so many completely unrelated conversations with so many completely unrelated widows within one short week, reinforcing my belief that, different though we may be in every other way, we are similar in our widowhood.

Widow 1: I went to get a flu shot at the City Department of Public Health. Unlike other years, private doctors were getting the vaccine after almost everyone else, and word had leaked out that the city had a supply. There, in a teeming sea of little children who needed vaccines of various kinds, I ran into an old friend, a friend I had been wanting to visit with all summer. This was our opportunity to chat, and chat we did. She has been a widow for sixteen years, and in all that time she has never discussed with me how she felt about being alone. Why we began to talk of our widowhood, I am not sure, but she told me of recent travails, in the context of her aloneness. She had had open-heart surgery while she was vacationing in Florida, followed by weeks of complications, and her children shuttled from their homes and families across the country to be of support. When my brother and I did that for my mother after she had her heart attack in Florida many years ago, I learned that it is much worse to be the one to uproot your children's lives than to be the family members so uprooted. Just the week before, she had had a minor car accident, with all the attendant aggravations—insurance, rental car, a fine to pay. She was upbeat about it all (she is a very cheerful person), but she confessed that to handle it alone is a big, fat pain.

She also told me about an article she had read some while ago, about a woman who feels that there is someone in the house with her—a wrinkled old woman, she thinks. As the writer of the article describes it, the woman in the house catches glimpses of this "intruder" and sees her reflection in a window as she passes, or in the reflective glass of a picture, even sometimes in the shiny bottom of a pan. And then she knows. She is seeing her own reflection, not the one in the mirror when she is putting on her makeup or adjusting her sweater. *This* old woman is the person the world sees when they look at her and she never even knew it.

Widow 2 and Widow 3: After I got my shot, I went shopping. Shopping has never been my favorite pastime, but this particular afternoon it seemed as if it might be a pick-me-up. As I was standing at the cash register, I overheard two nice-looking, kind of familiar-looking women talking to each other as they looked at the skirts and jackets.

"I went to Florida last year but I really didn't enjoy it. I'm not going back this year," one said to the other.

"I know I won't be able to go this winter," her friend answered, with a sob in her voice. "How long has it been for you?" she asked.

"It will be two years next month," said the first woman. And now I did recognize the woman who was about to speak and knew what she was going to say as she wiped her eyes, "George died just three months ago," and her friend said, "I know, I know."

Widow 4: This widow is an old, old friend to whom I speak often and intimately. I know when she is having bad days, and many days of the last four years have been bad. Her husband's death was long and lingering; her own health is not so great; she cannot drive after dark—the whole ball of wax. And last week she was sick again, and in this phone call she said, straight out and plain, "I am depressed and lonely and I just need G." What we need, we cannot have. Our husbands.

Widow 5: What she said to me was, "It's been six years and I am beginning to forget R, not forget everything about him, but it is getting harder and harder to remember what life used to be like. I'm forgetting the person I was then, the person he was. I need to be able to bring him back. Of course I cannot *bring him back*, but I am losing even his voice, his being—him. As soon as he died, I immediately became someone else, someone bunched-in with all the other widows. Now I even find that I am thrust with people that were not especially friends of mine before but because we are widows together, we are supposed to spend time together."

Widow 6: This is a woman we should all emulate. In the online book group, we had decided that a little autobiographical background would help round out the picture we have presented of ourselves. I am finding that most of my "geezerettes" are in their sixties and early seventies. I thought I would win the oldest-in-show-and-tell, but a wonderful post came from a constant reader and poster, who definitely wins. She writes:

I was born 1912, so that makes me older than everybody in here . . . in Czechoslovakia. My husband and I came to the USA in 1941 from Germany with the last ship before the war with Japan. We had our baby who was 10 months old and were not allowed a thing to take with us . . . so we had a very hard beginning, but everything turned out fine. 6 months later we had a baby girl. Both my husband and I were working and were able to send the children to college.

My dear husband passed away 13 years ago and I have 4 grandchildren and 2 ggchildren and they are the apple of my eye. I have hobbies like crocheting, sewing, exercising, crossword puzzles and playing Scrabble with the computer . . . also do volunteer work and love to read. So there you have it . . . my daughter lives in Wisconsin, but my son and his family live ½ hour away from me. I see him every Sunday.

Finally, two remarkable women who do win the Ninety and Over category for me. One just had a ninetieth birthday, the other is close to ninety-nine, and visiting with them is pure pleasure. They are bright and enthusiastic, interested and interesting. M. has always had a self-deprecating, but slightly wicked sense of humor, laughing at herself but with a rare insight into the foibles of all of us. The reason for our long talk recently was that she called to thank me for a few flowers I had sent for her birthday, and this gave me a chance to tell her how much I admired her, her unselfish commitment to her family, to the needs of others, and her courage in facing the death of a son in a tragic accident years ago. "I was afraid I was going to lose it then," she said. "But, of course, I couldn't . . . for Doc" (her husband). She recognized that a good marriage made for an easier widowhood, an idea to which not everyone would subscribe, but I agreed. I do agree most heartily.

E. is physically limited, with a weakening heart and loss of vision, but she is still beautiful, sharp, and alert. Once she was a voracious reader, with books piled beside her chair; now she listens to books on tape and talks not only about the books but about the news and Ohio State sports with real enthusiasm and knowledge. She was an excellent golfer, with the most fluid of swings, and I never could beat her. I remember standing on the eighth green at the country club so many years ago, wishing, wishing that she would miss her putt instead of thinking, thinking how I could sink mine! We don't exactly have control of how we age, but these two nonagenarians tell us something worth remembering about attitude.

In 1995, in America, elderly women outnumbered elderly men three to two; in the eighty-five and older group, there were five women for every man; and among the 9.8 million individuals age sixty-five and older who live alone, fully 77 percent, nearly eight out of ten, were women. All shapes, all sizes, all colors, all ethnicities, all kinds of emotions. Just that same old common denominator. Just other widows.

For a Sprained Ankle, a Frozen Package of Peas

$\mathscr{B}$ECAUSE OF my steep driveway—in my mind always the *damndriveway*—I often pick up my mail when I am returning home. I have gotten very adept at pulling up close enough to the mailbox to retrieve my mail without having to get out of the car and without knocking the box off the post. Putting the mail on the seat beside me, however, practically guarantees that it will slide to the floor before I get to the garage. When the mail is a pile of catalogs (isn't the mail always a pile of catalogs?), I pick them up from the floor and throw most of them in the trash before I open the door into the house. If Bloomingdale's and Saks and Sharper Image knew how seldom

I read them, would they continue to write me day after day after day?

Last week, though, what fell to the floor was a little packet of cards; the packaging made it intriguing enough to bring into the house. I opened the packet to unveil a veritable deck of items available through Maturity.com, with the catchy subtitle "Laugh, cry, think, learn and click." I looked at all those little cards and I cried before I laughed, and I didn't learn a thing. This is what they were selling: Pride Scooters; Prescription Plus Pharmacy for Diabetics . . . and Medicare Patients with Impotence Problems; Catholic Cemeteries; New Soft Hearing Aids; Affordable Funeral and Cremation Care; Adult Day Care Programs, with a specialized program for Alzheimer's; the new Rampvan, "the ultimate wheelchair-friendly mini van"; and a home delivery service for Depends.

We are the graying of America; we are a major market. Who am I to think that Renata hearing-aid batteries should not be a mouse-click away? Of course, they should—I just don't want all that "in sickness" part of the marriage vow cluttering up my mailbox. (In fairness to Dr. Leonard of the well-established *Dr. Leonard's*, America's leading discount health care catalog, Bob did order some pretty clever items that helped him after his back surgery to put his socks on and take them off again.)

In my generation, marriage vows were not taken lightly. Formal divorce was rare, so there were plenty of unhappy couples living under the same roof until death did them part. Times have changed. I make no judgment. Those academics who write the reports based on statistics can prove it any way they wish to interpret the data. What I know for certain is when I was sick, my husband cared for me. He brought orange juice to my bed when I had a cold; he sat . . . and sat . . . and sat . . . in the emergency room when I had a heart attack. For a widow in a house alone, to have even a terrible cold is scary.

One of my friends developed severe shingles the week her husband died. Not only were they painful, they were directly under her left shoulder blade, a place she could not reach with the cream that gave her some relief. Another friend badly sprained her ankle and was ordered to stay off her feet. There was no one to bring her the family-sized packages of frozen peas that she needed to get from the freezer every few hours to put on her ankle. (This is a tip worth remembering. Those big bags of peas conform better to the shape of an ankle than an ice bag.) I had a stupid accident one rainy Sunday morning at 5:00 A.M. as I was going into the bathroom. I stumbled (I could hear Bob's voice: "Why didn't you put the light on?") and I cut my arm, quite deeply, on the handle of the toilet. I knew I should go to the emergency room for stitches. I also knew I wasn't going. Clumsily, since I can't put adhesive on my skin (hence I had no super-large Band-Aid), I tried wrapping gauze around the wound, dripping a little blood on the carpet of the dressing room as I tried different maneuvers to anchor one end of the gauze.

But that was just a warm-up for what happened next. It could be a book all on its own and I could call it *Just Another Widow Goes to the Hospital*. Like the "Honeybunch" series of yore, I could creatively come up with *Just Another Widow Goes on a Cruise* . . . or takes up yoga . . . or has a facelift. I have yet to try any of those adventures, but I certainly can give a firsthand report of what it is like to have a hospital experience pretty much alone . . . at least until you can notify your family.

Mercury in Retrograde

I REALLY DON'T believe in the occult, or even in the horoscope's predictions, but I sometimes think there is something mysterious in the alignment of the stars, and that Mercury in retrograde can create a force field that we don't quite understand.

Armistice Day weekend, one more holiday on which I couldn't honor Bob's service to his country because I couldn't reach the flag mount beside the front door, I punished myself by going to the grocery. Maybe that's a little exaggeration, but going to the grocery does not lift my spirits. Even when I was shopping to provide for the well-being of my whole family, I did not feel rewarded—but, at least, this weekend I was planning to provide, once again, for some of my family. Tim was coming for Thanksgiving with Tucker and Hannah. The turkey dinner was going to be at Debby's, but I needed to lay in a supply of soft drinks and snacks, think ahead to lunches and a couple of regular dinners, mix my famous cream cheese and black olive spread, which the kids devour on saltines. Wede as Emeril.

Walking through Kroger's, unconsciously leaning on the grocery cart, I collected items that had not entered my head until I saw them: cans of soup, bottles of wine, peanut butter and pickles, huge packages of toilet paper. As I waited at the checkout counter, my head felt light and my legs felt like rubber. I wanted to stop by the in-store bank and cash a check, but I couldn't make it. I went home via the bank drive-through window, and got the car with the groceries into the garage. It took me the entire day to move them into the kitchen: the Dove bars to the freezer, the vegetables to the refrigerator, the multiple jars and boxes and cans to their proper shelves. I would bring a bag, sit for a half hour, then bring another bag. In between trips, I watched the disastrous Ohio State–Michigan game. My evaluation of myself: I am tired.

Sunday evening, Lois and I had planned to go to a nice seafood restaurant for dinner. She was scheduled for a cataract operation the next morning. A friend of ours, who would be up early to leave on an Arts Center–sponsored bus trip, was to drop her at the outpatient eye surgery; her brother was to be phoned when she was ready to go home. I had planned to relieve him at Lois's house until the help she had lined up to stay overnight arrived. What a lonely proposition.

The plan that evening was for me to follow Lois to the Mercury dealership, where she was leaving her car to be serviced during the days she wouldn't be driving, and then we would go on to the restaurant in my car. As she pulled her car up to the service bay and dropped her keys and instructions into the box, I looked around that dark and cold and empty lot and thought about how, when you are eighty-one and alone, you do manage, in a way that you could not have imagined or contemplated. When she got into my car and we were driving out I said something to her that she and I do not talk about. I said, "This is kind of pathetic, isn't it—two old ladies on a cold winter's night, doing what we are doing?" And then we went to Fisherman's Wharf for dinner.

We did have divine crab cakes. As we were leaving, I had that light-headed, weak-kneed feeling again, plus being nauseated. I had a decision to make: What would be the more dangerous drive home? Me sick or Lois visually impaired? After changing seats, in which move she lost one good leather glove, Lois drove us home slowly and well, got out at her own house, and I made the short drive home with no problem. Bed felt good, and I almost dismissed it from my mind.

Monday morning I was due to have my pro-time checked at the doctor's office to see if my Coumaden dosage was correct and thought I would be remiss not to mention the little weekend episodes. I should have known that conscientious and careful as they are at that office, there would be no leaving until I was completely checked out. What blood tests and an EKG revealed was that I was fibrillating wildly and that I was bleeding internally. "We have a potentially serious problem here," said my doctor, seriously. "I'm going to put you in the hospital." All I could think was, "Oh hell . . . there couldn't be a worse time!"

On Sunday morning Debby had left on a much-anticipated trip to California to take Maggie to a spa for a few days of mother-daughter catch-up. They were both so excited, and I was so excited for them. Debby's new book, *One Memory at a Time*, had just been published; Maggie had a new job lined up, Tim was in Colorado, working especially hard, and Bob was in Florida on business. I was, until "potentially serious" showed up, under the false impression that the Greenes, one and all, were in pretty good shape. And now here I was, in a doctor's examining room, waiting to hear if my next move was to the hospital (if Admitting could even find space for me).

I drove the two minutes home from the doctor's, and while I waited to hear if there was a bed—hopefully one where I could be hooked up to telemetry—I called Tim and Bob, just to alert them, trying hard not to scare them. I knew they would be alarmed if they phoned over the course of a day or two and could not reach me, and knew that for the time being, I didn't have to worry Debby. She was in a car somewhere between L.A. and Palm Springs. The other person I didn't want to alert or alarm was my wonderful brother, who was due to leave Tuesday morning for a Florida Thanksgiving with his family. How many people's plans can one woman screw up? Too damned many.

I had been home less than an hour when the doctor's office called. There was a room; the nurse told me I was to be adamant in Admitting that I did not need to go through the emergency room process but was to go immediately to the arranged-for room. Very fortunately my lovely next-door neighbor was home, and she came immediately and took me to the proper desk. She was much too familiar with the layout and procedures of Mt. Carmel East. Her husband had also been fibrillating, and had just gotten a pacemaker the week before. The corner of Rock Hill and Revere seemed to be the fibrillating center of it all.

My maternal grandmother, born near the middle of the nineteenth century, told my mother, who then told me, that above the door of every hospital it should be writ large: *"Abandon hope all ye who enter here."*

Dante might have said it first, but my Nana appropriated it to reflect her experiences. Times haven't changed all that much. Now, you don't so much abandon hope as comfort, dignity, and any sense of control. I was a lucky patient, who found herself in the capable hands of marvelous, young specialists who began to work miracles. But still.

At the Admitting desk, the staff person asked me who was with me and I had to say "nobody." She thought that was "awesome," which made me tell her that I was writing a book and this experience was going to make one great chapter. So they wheelchaired me up to Room 280, and the next part of the chapter was under way.

It involved a lot of repetition: test after test, the same medical history to aide, to nurse, to intern, to resident. By the time I had been there three hours, my chart was an inch thick. After Tuesday, it was two inches thick, increasing exponentially each day thereafter.

Meanwhile, my brother, of course, came to the hospital. Before I could convince him otherwise, he changed his Florida ticket. He was going to stay in town until Wednesday and see how things were going. How they were going on Tuesday was inconclusive. I needed more tests. Al, once again, negotiated with Delta to get him out of Columbus on Thursday morning, while Bob, in Florida, was working the airlines to get here on Wednesday evening.

In the interim, I had reached Debby and Maggie at the spa, so at least we could talk daily, but I knew that my being in the hospital was not part of the relaxation package they had signed up for.

Al and I actually had a great visit over the three days. He came in the morning, and in the afternoon and in the evening. I had a nice, private room that no one would ever confuse with The Four Seasons, or even my own bedroom, but it was an intimate time, reminiscent of days we had spent together in Florida when our mother had had a heart attack and was in intensive care, awaiting a pacemaker! Talk about the gene pool! Al and I are siblings who love each other without reservation and that's a gene that is not in everyone's DNA.

Sometime in the night, Tuesday, I got up, went to the bathroom and went comfortably back to bed, I thought. When I next came to, all the lights in the room were blazing, I was hooked to an EKG machine, the room was full of personnel of all varieties, and the nurse, Jill, who had seen me safely to bed earlier was patting my head and saying "You scared me to death." It seems that my heart rate had dropped to 30, the monitor in the nurses' station went off, and when Jill came running into my room, there was nobody home. Twice. Technically, they called it an apneac attack. In the vernacular, I was a Code Blue. I had not seen that famous golden glow that you are supposed to see when you have a near-death experience, but I knew I had been in the hands of the Lord to be in that place at that time.

Many consults consulted with each other and the conclusion became obvious. The multitudes of medicines I had been taking since my heart surgery eight years before and for the more recent fibrillation had caused the bleeding into my stomach. The decision was made to cut down on the medication and get my heart rate less erratic with a pacemaker. I could hardly wait. The surgery had been scheduled to be a late-afternoon "add-on," but for some reason was moved to an early morning "start-with." I had changed my in-case-of-emergency contact from Al to Bob. Before 7:00 A.M. the nurse called him to come a runnin'; he was there to meet the surgeon as soon as I was ready to go back to my room. I had another chance for an unanticipated visit with him for a day. Debby got home Thursday night and came straight from the airport to the hospital. We shed a few tears.

My offspring and I waited all morning for two doctors to sign my release. I think I know how a prisoner feels waiting for the parole board. I kept being afraid there would be some hitch. By noon, the paperwork was done and I was wheeled to the proper exit where Debby was to pick me up. Once again, as we drove out, I was blindsided by the memory of many times taking that exact drive, down from the parking garage to where Bob, in the wheelchair, was waiting for me to take him home and lavish him with love and attention.

For a widow, and her children, we had, as Bob so often said, dodged another bullet. Although it has so many medical implications, I mean this to be an optimistic report, a constructive story. It proves the higher the hurdle, the higher we can jump. My Angina Monologue.

And as soon as Lois could drive after her cataract operation, she went back to the Fisherman Wharf's parking lot and there, in the rainy leaves, was her good leather glove. Mercury had had a chance to come out of retrograde.

Memorials, Public and Private

$\mathcal{T}$HE FIRST TIME I ever talked to Tom Hanks or, really, the first time Tom Hanks ever talked to me was to ask for a contribution for the World War II memorial. Another veteran's widow, whose husband's navy service was in dirigibles, told me how to call an 800 number to reach Tom and make a pledge. I think if I had had to make a choice between eating and making the donation, I would have chosen the donation. The wartime service of the currently well-publicized greatest generation is very much au courant now, but let another decade or so go by, without a major monument, and we—actually they, those who wore the uniform—might become the forgotten generation. I was a war bride, living in Oregon for a year and a half before Bob went overseas, and loving it. A newly minted second lieutenant and his bride, with all those other newly minted officers, fresh from Fort Benning and Officers Training School . . . all on their own, no family obligations, no traditional rules for holidays, no requisite calls or visits, just new faces to turn into new friends. There was a group of us who gravitated toward each other, who gravitated toward Bob. For the wives, it was glamorous in its simplicity: backyard picnics, weekends at Crater Lake, and one memorable trip to Bend, Oregon, for me, to an elegant lodge while the 91st Division was on maneuvers. For the men, of course, there was no glamour, only very hard work to make the 91st Division a fighting unit before being sent to Africa and then Italy. There was one famous story that I'm sure was not apocryphal, when the men, on a ninety-one-mile hike, passed by General Gerhardt, reviewing the exhausted infantrymen from his horse. His young son is reported to have said, "Make 'em run, Daddy. I want to hear their mess kits rattle." Gerhardt was compared, by *Time* magazine, to General George Patton. The troops certainly felt that way.

Raising the money for the memorial seems to have been very difficult, because, as expected, there was controversy over its design and placement. Bob Dole is now the honorary chair of the fund-raising effort and it has finally been approved for the spot it deserves, on the National Mall between the Washington Monument and the Lincoln Memorial. I had a letter from Schoedinger's that the funeral directors across America have committed themselves to a nationwide fund-raising goal of $5 million to help construct the memorial. I think of the numbers of veterans' widows in their files, the number of funerals where the triangularized flag has been presented. At Bob's, the flag in a wooden case was on a table in the room where we greeted those who had come to pay their respects. How I wish that their grandfather, the Major, could have seen his two twelve-year-old grandsons, without anyone having suggested it, standing at parade rest, feet apart, hands folded behind their backs on either side of his flag.

Bob and I never did get to Washington to see the Vietnam Memorial. The traveling Wall did come to Columbus and we went, to stand in line, crying, with the hundreds of others who were there that hot Sunday afternoon. I would hope that some kind of replica of this new memorial will be built to be sent around the country for me and the thousands and thousands of widows for whom December 12 is a personal commemoration for the heroes of our lives.

Needing My (Cyber)Space

$\mathcal{I}$T WAS PROBABLY twenty years ago that my then son-in-law gave me the most wonderful Christmas present. It was a little, really little, computer called a Timex Sinclair 1000, and a book about developing a computer called *The Soul of a New Machine* by Tracy Kidder. What a revelation. What knowledge. I was ready to pack for a journey. I didn't even know where I was headed, but it was going to be special and I was going to lead the pack, if only I could understand the way this was supposed to work. First off, it seemed that all the information should be *in* the contraption, like it seems to be in the TV. Why did I have to feed those cassette tapes into it before I could even start? How could I even have understood the concept of storing data? I do think that it only had three or four functions: an address book, a calendar, and a calculator. Nevertheless, I was enthralled, and found a computer-savior in the most unlikely of places.

Not far from where we lived there was a drugstore in the basement of a suburban medical office building, and through whatever stroke of luck, I found out that the pharmacist-owner was a Timex buff. It was not a pharmacy I used, but I was running over to it constantly, luring him away from filling prescriptions to give me helpful hints. (Columbus being Columbus, Gary is now with the CVS pharmacy that I do use and where he is much too often filling my prescriptions.)

Once I had mastered the art of this new machine, it finally began to dawn on me that what I'd learned was what there was, and it wasn't enough. For the following three Christmases, Bob gave me a gift certificate for a Tandy computer at Radio Shack with the understanding that I would actually take possession of the computer after we came home from Florida and could take advantage of the instruction they offered. Three times I asked for a credit return. There was too much else I needed to do and my enthusiasm had moved back to real life: children, grandchildren, friends, and the community.

Enter the Macintosh. What was it about the apple with the bite (byte?) out of it that was so intriguing? It made me, once again, want my place in cyberspace, and I invested in my first Mac. This book is being written on my third Apple and once I am sure that the project is finished, I am going to treat myself to an iMac, a carrot-apple I have dangled in front of me to keep me moving ahead. Though I am more proficient than when I first began, I don't want to attempt moving any files from anywhere. I am truly afraid to switch computers in midwork; what if I lost what I have reported so far!!!

Bob was not thrilled with my enchanting toy. He didn't want to learn how to use it; he wasn't overjoyed that I was computer preoccupied, and he didn't like not being able to use the phone when I was online. So, throw the expense of a second line into the mix, the fact that when we were with friends I talked about my new fascination too much, and I would see that "enough already" look on his face. The only really good thing I did with my "skill" was widely inflate our net worth as I tried to enter our financial records. That bubble burst almost immediately as Bob compared real numbers to virtual numbers.

I am in love with the wonders of the Internet. I have bought bedspreads and cookies. I have learned about stenosis and Siam. They know me at Amazon, and I can access all the news all the time from all over the world. To have a list of favorite places is to have hours of pleasure and knowledge right in a box on your desk. Because we have a wonderful library system, I have been ordering books through the computer for a long time. Now the library has developed the most comprehensive of websites. I, who originally felt that it was a crime against learning to forsake the Dewey decimal system, now can appreciate what an on-screen database offers.

Computers are a miracle. A miracle that can be misused, not only for the obvious pornography openly available but for the ever-more prevalent request for e-mail addresses on all applications and the unending list of forwarded jokes that greet all of us daily.

Nevertheless, as we have entered this new century, I am beginning to feel like that person with the Timex. The multitude of new products, none of which I can comprehend, has my eighty-one-year-old head spinning. Do I need faster access? Road Runner and Earthlink look intriguing, but I can sacrifice time if it means I will no longer have access to AOL and my book group. But consider that AOL and Time Warner will soon merge and they should have their own high-speed cable connection. What about cell phones? In my car, I have the basic Model T version. I have it only for semi-emergencies and I am among the growing band of citizens who resent cellphone users' selfish assumption that their communicating needs transcend the rights of all the rest of us. Just last week, I was in a doctor's waiting room where a Rabbi (a *Rabbi!*) was making a real estate deal on his cell phone, surrounded by the worried and ailing. But how long can I resist 1,625 minutes for just $12.50 a month, plus a free phone, or 1,500 minutes, including long distance for only $34.99 a month or a $50 free merchandise card with a wireless phone purchase, especially when you might be dazzled by the merchandise. Dazzled but frazzled. VCRs still pose a major problem, and now we are onto DVD. Our record player was one generation past the Victrola and, out of the blue, here come compact discs. And Palm Pilots and pagers and scanners and pocket PCs and devices that can take photos and music from the computer. Will I ever catch up?

I don't even know what broadband is but the television advertising says that Enron is selling broadband width like commodities. Like the New York Stock Exchange, does that mean? EMC storage, "where information lives," sponsors a golf tournament. Bob Hope is supposed to sponsor golf tournaments or, as a reach, Cadillac at the Masters. Sun is the "dot in dot com," a meaningless concept even to those of who use it every day.

Not too long ago, I was heartened to read an ad for the aging (or any) motorist. It features a banner that says: PLEASE CALL POLICE. How low tech, how helpful, how timeless, how refreshing.

The Blue Room

 $\mathscr{M}$ Y HUSBAND DIED more than two years ago. Sometimes I feel as if ten years have passed and sometimes it feels like last week. So much has happened in the world around me, and actually, the changes in me are astonishing. I have made the first steps in the journey of widowhood, and I think I am stronger and as self-reliant as I had expected to be. I am used to my own company much of the time, and I'm not too bad a companion to be around. I accept who I am now and I can handle it. Amen.

I think it was my constant anchor, Dan Rather, who reported that every day one thousand World War II veterans die. Our son Bob has called it "the whisper of a generation saying good-bye to its children." One thousand veterans every day! I wish I knew the 999 other widows who are dreading December 12. I wish I knew how they were faring. I wish we could compare notes on this experience we have shared. I wish we could comfort each other. What a day we have to remember.

I am better. How do I know? For the first time, when I think about getting something accomplished, I do it. All those months ago, when Bob was first sick, the light fixture in the kitchen broke. In the fifteen minutes I felt that I could leave the house, I bought a horrible and gloomy replacement—so horrible and gloomy that, rather than eat in that light, I have carried my dinner to the sitting room where I kind of eat off the arm of the chair. Finally, the electrician came and installed a lovely, bright light. Like so much else that I accomplish, all credit goes to my daughter, who not only urges me on but saw the new fixture and sent me to the store.

And I am redecorating the sitting room into an up-to-date computer/TV room with new furniture, a reupholstered chair, and even new carpeting. Once again, I might still be dragging my feet if it hadn't been for Debby. A year ago, with all the urging in the world, I could not have gotten off the dime. The room is going to be blue, my favorite color . . . an upbeat, happy blue that will make me upbeat and happy. One whole wall behind the computer desk is covered with pictures of my family: the children then, the children as adults, the grandchildren at every stage. I counted and there are forty-four differ-ent photos. The computer table is such a beauty, a place for everything and everything in its place. On the table, right angled to the computer, are pictures of Bob, of Bob and me, framed in a red-leather heart. On that wall I have a lovely oil painting that had been my mother's, of white roses in a glass vase against a blue background, and there is a plaque that Debby gave me that says "Bidden or not bidden, God is present." This truly is a room of my own, the kind of nest we all need to make for ourselves. I am so thrilled to have it all here. My space.

More than that, I can now think about Bob as I want to remember him, not bedridden, not miserable, not in pain. Last night I awoke at about 2:00 a.m., as I often do, but unlike other nights, I tried to stay awake rather than wish myself back to sleep. For the next hour, I remembered fun and funny times, places we had been, friends with whom we had shared vacations and nights on the town and laughs—lots of laughs—and I warmed myself in the glow.

So I know I am going to be okay. Never the me that was, but the me who still has the capacity to function successfully and, yes, happily.

I have even negotiated a new car deal.

The Dow may be ending the year down for the first time in ten years, but the Tao, for day 365 says:

> *Turn the wheel of your life*
> *Make complete revolutions*
> *Celebrate every turning*
> *Persevere with joy.*

My only hope for those of you who read this is that your loneliness and sorrow will abate (it never goes away), and that you will soon be on your way to creating a Blue Room of your own.

Moonglow over
WY, WI, IN, OH, NY, LA, IL, PA, MA, NE, AZ, CA…

Writing *Moonglow* was a magnificent surprise for me. By putting my simple, everyday thoughts about widowhood on paper, I lightened the burden in my own heart and struck a chord in the hearts of my fellow citizens all over the country (and in Canada and England, as well). How truly humbled I have been by the response, and how many new friends I have made! Most of the letters began "Dear Phyllis," and that made me glad. Countless of their stories have been of loss and illnesses and caretaking of husbands and wives, parents and grandparents. Some of the letter writers, still happily married with a long, full life ahead, wrote to say that the words brought them up short, made them recognize life's blessings. Those letters brought me joy.

I have tried to answer each and every e-mail and those correspondences that came "on the snail," as we say in our online book group. I am so lucky to feel as if I now know all the people who wrote; I wish they all could know each other. We do have so much in common, and we are on this journey together. I wish, too, that I could reprint all of the letters. Wise, funny, articulate, heartbroken, brave, and accepting friends, I salute you.

What follows is a small sampling of the hundreds and hundreds of beautiful notes and letters, with my gratitude and very best wishes for the years ahead.

Dear Phyllis,

I have just finished reading your book *It Must Have Been Moonglow* and I felt compelled to write to you to let you know how much I appreciated it. I am not a widow. In fact, we may share very little in common. I am a thirty-two-year-old woman, happily married for twelve years, mother of three children, and I own and operate a small business. I picked up your book this week and in reading it I realized that death or major life changes are not something to fear, but rather events that we learn to walk through, learning as we go. I admire in you your strength of character when faced with obvious difficulties. Your writing was so honest, not sugar-coating the hardship of it, but letting others know that you can keep going, and that there can be a full measure of joy in our journey.

I do not pretend to have a way of expressing myself well. In fact, I can count on one hand the number of times that I've actually written a letter of this type. I just wanted to tell you that I enjoyed your

book and I would think that it could be a great help
to those going through similar circumstances.

Sincerely,
Barbara

Hello, Phyllis.

My name is Amanda. I lost my husband on
11/23/01. He was a police officer and was providing
back-up to another officer when he lost control of his
cruiser . . . and was killed. He blessed me with one
son, Samuel (seventeen months old).

I received your book soon after the funeral. I can't
even tell you who got it for me, if it was left in my mailbox, on my front porch, or if it was hand-delivered.

I have had it on my dresser ever since that day and
never had any intentions of reading it. You had fifty-
six years with your husband, I was married to Jerry
for four. How in the world could I relate my suffering
to yours? Well, one night while I wasn't sleeping and
should have been, I picked the darn book up—and I
couldn't put it down.

I definitely wasn't reading about my life, but I was

reading about my feelings. I have connected with so many of the things you talk about in your book. So many that I can't even list them.

So, I just wanted to thank you. Your words seemed to just pour into me and I am touched. I know that I'm going to be okay too.

Respectfully yours,
Amanda Wyss
Decatur, IN

I picked up your book at my grandmother's house the other day and began to read. I felt an overwhelming need to thank you. I am thirty-five, married, the mother of two (three-year-old girl, eighteen-month-old boy). I, thankfully, know nothing about widowhood.

As I read your description of Bob, I saw my own husband in my mind's eye. I saw him, as you see your Bob, in our backyard, tanned, healthy, and happy. Thank you. We've been so busy with work and with the children that I think I may have forgotten just how much I love him.

As I read about your grocery shopping for one, I saw myself complaining about the shopping, the dishes, meal preparation, etc. Thank you. I think I may have forgotten that these are the days.

I'm sure you wrote the book for women like my grandmother, but I hope you realize that you made a stay-at-home mom in Alabama open her eyes a little wider today. I cooked dinner tonight with a little more zest, and I hugged my kids a little harder. I haven't felt this fuzzy in a long time! I've been lost in the day to day. Thanks for the map!

Beth Leva
Lanett, AL

Dear Phyllis,

. . . I've been widowed twice. . . . Whatever the age we are widowed, so many of the feelings are similar. I must admit it's taken longer for me to recover this time. This spring of 2002 (five and a half years after Don's death) finally feels like "I'm coming back." I've cleaned the closet, repaired the broken window in the sun house, finally bought the shades for the den . . . who would ever believe it takes so long to get things done. Until now I've just thought I was sheer laziness incarnate!! But, in time, just like after losing Norm, something "clicked." I'm not sure what, I guess we really can't define it. I just know that it's different. Oh, I still turn on the TV or the radio for "company," but I can sit in the quiet and read a book again. I can't tell you how long before I could even read a book . . . and even now I look for "little" ones!!! My lack of concentration was formidable. I don't know if you are familiar with our local humorist, Loretta LaRoche, but I feel like shouting her line: "I'm b-a-a-a-a-ack!"

I'm so grateful for "blue room" time. I know we must find it for ourselves and no one else can get us here . . . your book is a dear affirmation. Thanks so much for sharing.

Hugs,
Fran Jewers Langille
Worcester, MA

Dear Mrs. Greene:

. . . I have been widowed for just over eighteen months. My wife of fifty-three years, Beryl, died very suddenly of what was diagnosed as an aortic dissection. She was right in the middle of so many activities and was gone in a microsecond. I suppose I will never get over it. But your book has helped me. You say so many things that touch me and I know exactly what they mean. I responded to your comments on the computer. I don't know how I would have got through this terrible time without it. I have my group of cyberwidows (we use our real names and addresses)—they are from all over the States and one in Canada and another in Australia. They have been so wonderful that last year we arranged a get together in North Carolina. It was just for a long weekend but it was amazing how well we got along—as if we had known each other for months. So I was the lone man with ten widows (several who communicate by e-mail could not be there). . . . We made quite a show in restaurants—one man with these ladies ranging in age from twenty-eight to maybe sixty-five. I find that writing my thoughts down does

help. I won't call it "healing" (I hate that word) but it does help.

My best wishes,

from seventy-eight-year-old Tom Smith,

who has a pain in his heart: . . .Coupeville, WA

Dear Phyllis,

I became a widow last December for the second time. Once at forty and again at sixty-seven. I'm not happy to report that I haven't gotten any better at it. It must be age. The first time I had a nine-year-old daughter and was probably absorbed with getting her raised up and working on my career. Now things are much quieter with fewer friends around and less of a social life.

I just wanted to tell you how valuable your book is to me. The little stories make me realize that all of these things that happen every day are not just my trials and tribulations, but for all of us. It also makes me feel bad that I never understood how my mother must have felt when my father died at fifty-six, leav-

ing her with no work history or money—totally
dependent on us for all kinds of support. I am going
to loan your book to my daughter so she might
understand some of my feelings and give me the
breaks that I never gave my own mother. I think the
very best part of the book for me was the last. Right
now my memories of the last sixteen years with my
husband, Peter, although funny and happy and loving, are so painful. Your final chapter gives me hope
that sometime, maybe not soon but sometime, I will
be able to look back at them and feel the fun and the
happiness and love without the pain. Thanks so
much for sharing this little gem with me—and all the
rest of us out there.

Marjory Sgroi
Ashton-Drye Associates Tours
Buffalo, NY

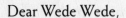

Dear Wede Wede,

I wrote to you a couple of weeks ago after reading
your book and said that I was planning to read it a second time. Well, I think some things are better the sec-

ond time around, and that is what I am finding with *It Must Have Been Moonglow.* I really enjoyed it the first reading, but now I am noting things that I missed.

One thing that really struck me was that, *we are a widow now and not a wife.* Frankly, I still have not learned to like the title "widow," however, when I must tell someone that I am not married, I am always quick to say that I am widowed, and not divorced. Just a preference I guess. However, just like you, I will always be PhyllisandBob in my own mind.

It is graduation time and in the past couple of weeks we had two granddaughters graduate from college and this week a grandson will graduate from high school. Oh how much I wish that Grandpa was here to enjoy these special times together. But I think he is watching from heaven with pride in his grandchildren.

I still have a few chapters to finish the book before I return it to my neighbor, with great thanks to her for lending it to me. (I really need to get a copy of my own.)

Have a great day, and blessings to you.

Shalom,

Phyllis J. Williams

Jenison, MI

———⟨——

Hello Phyllis Greene,

. . . I was widowed in 1996 at age forty-nine, after twenty-eight years of marriage, and since 1997 I have been director of the Emma Rogers Society here at MIT, which is an organization for widows of MIT faculty and alumni. My late husband was a graduate of MIT, class of 1967.

. . . MIT began this organization in 1990 to keep in touch with widows so that they in turn would keep in touch with MIT. We send out two newsletters a year, spring and fall, and also a widow's information packet. . . . We have programs here on campus twice a year, with faculty as speakers. . . . We also have activities during Reunion and Commencement weekend; widows are welcome to join in with their husband's class or participate with the Emma Rogers Society.

. . . I remarried last year, a widower, whom I met through family friendships. A totally unexpected but happy turn of events. I never would have imagined it happening, I was always busy living my "new" life, but we both feel blessed. The heartbreak of being widowed is a bond we share, although we don't dwell on it. But believe me, every day is precious, and we are grateful.

. . . I hope you are enjoying your beautiful Blue Room!

> Sincerely,
> Mary K. Speare
> Massachusetts Institute of Technology
> Cambridge, MA

Dear Mrs. Greene,

There were so many reasons I read your book! My grandparents are in their early (and young) eighties and still *so* much in love.

. . . After reading your book I realized a new view in my own two-year-old marriage. For this I cannot thank you enough. Oh how marriage is a gift to enjoy and love and laugh everyday.

. . . We are all souls wrapped in skin, no matter the

age of our skin, life throws us all these learning times and times of joy and sadness. Your book helped me realize this.

You have a friend in Denver, Colorado, who will keep you in her heart and prayers. (I pray I am as young as you when I am eighty-one!)

Fondly, Laura Brock
Denver, CO

PS: My grandmother that I mentioned is a war bride too. My grandparents were married in 1941 in Addison, Illinois. My grandpa was in the Navy. . . . My grandparents love to polka dance. My grandpa plays the "button box" while my grandma plays the "spoons"!

Phyllis Greene can be reached at:

6956 East Broad Street #173
Columbus, Ohio 43213

or wedewede@aol.com
or www.familyhistories.com